faith.

100 verses
for your
daily journey.

Freeman-Smith, a division of Worthy Media, Inc.

134 Franklin Road, Suite 200, Brentwood, Tennessee 37027

The quoted ideas expressed in this book (but not Scripture verses) are not, in all cases, exact quotations, as some have been edited for clarity and brevity. In all cases, the author has attempted to maintain the speaker's original intent. In some cases, quoted material for this book was obtained from secondary sources, primarily print media. While every effort was made to ensure the accuracy of these sources, the accuracy cannot be guaranteed. For additions, deletions, corrections, or clarifications in future editions of this text, please write Freeman-Smith.

Scripture quotations are taken from:

The Holy Bible, King James Version (KJV)

The Holy Bible, New International Version (NIV) Copyright © 1973, 1978, 1984, by International Bible Society. Used by permission of Zondervan Publishing House. All rights reserved.

The Holy Bible, New King James Version (NKJV) Copyright © 1982 by Thomas Nelson, Inc. Used by permission.

Holy Bible, New Living Translation, (NLT) copyright © 1996. Used by permission of Tyndale House Publishers, Inc., Wheaton, Illinois 60189. All rights reserved.

The Message (MSG)- This edition issued by contractual arrangement with NavPress, a division of The Navigators, U.S.A. Originally published by NavPress in English as THE MESSAGE: The Bible in Contemporary Language copyright 2002-2003 by Eugene Peterson. All rights reserved.

New Century Version®. (NCV) Copyright © 1987, 1988, 1991 by Word Publishing, a division of Thomas Nelson, Inc. All rights reserved. Used by permission.

The New American Standard Bible®, (NASB) Copyright © 1960, 1962, 1963, 1968, 1971, 1972, 1973, 1975, 1977, 1995 by The Lockman Foundation. Used by permission.

The Holman Christian Standard Bible™ (HCSB) Copyright © 1999, 2000, 2001 by Holman Bible Publishers. Used by permission.

Cover Design by Kim Russell / Wahoo Designs
Page Layout by Bart Dawson

ISBN 978-1-60587-353-4

faith.

100 verses
for your
daily journey.

Introduction

There are some Bible verses that are so important, so crucial to the Christian faith, that every believer should consider them carefully and review them often. This text examines 100 of the most familiar verses from God's Holy Word. These verses, which you've probably heard many times before, are short enough, and memorable enough, to provide faith and courage for your daily journey. So do yourself and your loved ones a favor: study each verse and do your best to place it permanently in your mind and in your heart. When you do, you'll discover that having God's Word in your heart is even better than having a Bible on your bookshelf.

If you have faith as a mustard seed, you will say to this mountain, "Move from here to there," and it will move; and nothing will be impossible for you.

Matthew 17:20 NKJV

Mountain-Moving Faith

Because we live in a demanding world, all of us have mountains to climb and mountains to move. Moving those mountains requires faith.

Are you a mountain mover whose faith is evident for all to see? Or, are you a spiritual shrinking violet? God needs more men and women who are willing to move mountains for His glory and for His kingdom.

Jesus taught His disciples that if they had faith, they could move mountains. You can too. When you place your faith, your trust, indeed your life in the hands of Christ Jesus, you'll be amazed at the marvelous things He can do. So strengthen your faith through praise, through worship, through Bible study, and through prayer. And trust God's plans. With Him, all things are possible, and He stands ready to open a world of possibilities to you . . . if you have faith.

Concentration camp survivor Corrie ten Boom relied on faith during her long months of imprisonment and torture. Later, despite the fact that four of her family members had died in Nazi death camps, Corrie's faith was unshaken. She wrote, "There is no pit so deep that God's love is not deeper still." Christians take note: Genuine faith in God means faith in all circumstances, happy or sad, joyful or tragic.

If your faith is being tested to the point of breaking, remember that your Savior is near. If you reach out to Him in faith, He will give you peace and strength. Reach out today. If you touch even the smallest fragment of the Master's garment, He will make you whole. And then, with no further ado, let the mountain moving begin.

I am truly grateful that faith enables me to move past the question of "Why?"

—

Zig Ziglar

More Great Ideas About Faith

Faith is seeing light with the eyes of your heart, when the eyes of your body see only darkness.

Barbara Johnson

Grace calls you to get up, throw off your blanket of helplessness, and to move on through life in faith.

Kay Arthur

The popular idea of faith is of a certain obstinate optimism: the hope, tenaciously held in the face of trouble, that the universe is fundamentally friendly and things may get better.

J. I. Packer

There are a lot of things in life that are difficult to understand. Faith allows the soul to go beyond what the eyes can see.

John Maxwell

When you enroll in the "school of faith," you never know what may happen next. The life of faith presents challenges that keep you going—and keep you growing!

Warren Wiersbe

If God chooses to remain silent, faith is content.

Ruth Bell Graham

This is the day which the LORD hath made; we will rejoice and be glad in it.

Psalm 118:24 KJV

Celebrate the Gift of Life

Today is a non-renewable resource—once it's gone, it's gone forever. Our responsibility, as thoughtful believers, is to use this day in the service of God's will and in the service of His people. When we do so, we enrich our own lives and the lives of those whom we love.

God has richly blessed us, and He wants you to rejoice in His gifts. That's why this day—and each day that follows—should be a time of prayer and celebration as we consider the Good News of God's free gift: salvation through Jesus Christ.

Oswald Chambers correctly observed, "Joy is the great note all throughout the Bible." E. Stanley Jones echoed that thought when he wrote, "Christ and joy go together." But, even the most dedicated Christians can, on occasion, forget to celebrate each day for what it is: a priceless gift from God.

What do you expect from the day ahead? Are you expecting God to do wonderful things, or are you living beneath a cloud of apprehension and doubt? The familiar words of Psalm 118:24 remind us that every day is a cause for celebration. Our duty, as believers, is to rejoice in God's marvelous creation.

Today, celebrate the life that God has given you. Today, put a smile on your face, kind words on your lips, and a song in your heart. Be generous with your praise and free with your encouragement. And then, when you have celebrated life to the fullest, invite your friends to do likewise. After all, this is God's day, and He has given us clear instructions for its use. We are commanded to rejoice and be glad.

Submit each day to God, knowing that He is God over all your tomorrows.

—

Kay Arthur

More Great Ideas About Joyful Living

If you can forgive the person you were, accept the person you are, and believe in the person you will become, you are headed for joy. So celebrate your life.

Barbara Johnson

As Christians, we must live a day at a time. No person, no matter how wealthy or gifted, can live two days at a time. God provides for us day by day.

Warren Wiersbe

When we truly walk with God throughout our day, life slowly starts to fall into place.

Bill Hybels

Yesterday is the tomb of time, and tomorrow is the womb of time. Only now is yours.

R. G. Lee

If we are ever going to be or do anything for our Lord, now is the time.

Vance Havner

For God so loved the world, that he gave his only begotten Son, that whosoever believeth in him should not perish, but have everlasting life.

John 3:16 KJV

The Gift of Eternal Life

John 3:16 is a verse that you've undoubtedly known since childhood. After all, this verse is, quite possibly, the most widely recognized sentence in the entire Bible. But even if you memorized this verse many years ago, you still need to make sure it's a verse that you can recite by heart.

John 3:16 makes this promise: If you believe in Jesus, you will live forever with Him in heaven. It's an amazing promise, and it's the cornerstone of the Christian faith.

Eternal life is not an event that begins when you die. Eternal life begins when you invite Jesus into your heart right here on earth. So it's important to remember that God's plans for you are not limited to the ups and downs of everyday life. If you've allowed Jesus to reign over your heart, you've already begun your eternal journey.

As mere mortals, our vision for the future, like our lives here on earth, is limited. God's vision is not burdened by such limitations: His plans extend throughout all eternity.

Let us praise the Creator for His priceless gift, and let us share the Good News with all who cross our paths. We return our Father's love by accepting His grace and by sharing His message and His love. When we do, we are blessed here on earth and throughout all eternity.

Teach us to set our hopes on heaven, to hold firmly to the promise of eternal life, so that we can withstand the struggles and storms of this world.

—

Max Lucado

More Great Ideas About Eternal Life

Your choice to either receive or reject the Lord Jesus Christ will determine where you spend eternity.

Anne Graham Lotz

If you are a believer, your judgment will not determine your eternal destiny. Christ's finished work on Calvary was applied to you the moment you accepted Christ as Savior.

Beth Moore

The damage done to us on this earth will never find its way into that safe city. We can relax, we can rest, and though some of us can hardly imagine it, we can prepare to feel safe and secure for all of eternity.

Bill Hybels

God's salvation comes as gift; it is eternal, and it is a continuum, meaning it starts when I receive the gift in faith and is never-ending.

Franklin Graham

The one who is from God listens to God's words. This is why you don't listen, because you are not from God.

John 8:47 HCSB

Listening to God

Sometimes God speaks loudly and clearly. More often, He speaks in a quiet voice—and if you are wise, you will be listening carefully when He does. To do so, you must carve out quiet moments each day to study His Word and sense His direction.

Can you quiet yourself long enough to listen to your conscience? Are you attuned to the subtle guidance of your intuition? Are you willing to pray sincerely and then to wait quietly for God's response? Hopefully so. Usually God refrains from sending His messages on stone tablets or city billboards. More often, He communicates in subtler ways. If you sincerely desire to hear His voice, you must listen carefully, and you must do so in the silent corners of your quiet, willing heart.

More Great Ideas About Listening to God

In the soul-searching of our lives, we are to stay quiet so we can hear Him say all that He wants to say to us in our hearts.

Charles Swindoll

We cannot experience the fullness of Christ if we do all the expressing. We must allow God to express His love, will, and truth to us.

Gary Smalley

An essential condition of listening to God is that the mind should not be distracted by thoughts of resentment, ill-temper, hatred or vengeance, all of which are comprised in the general term, the wrath of man.

R. V. G. Tasker

When we come to Jesus stripped of pretensions, with a needy spirit, ready to listen, He meets us at the point of need.

Catherine Marshall

In prayer, the ear is of first importance. It is of equal importance with the tongue, but the ear must be named first. We must listen to God.

S. D. Gordon

And the peace of God, which surpasses every thought, will guard your hearts and your minds in Christ Jesus. Finally brothers, whatever is true, whatever is honorable, whatever is just, whatever is pure, whatever is lovely, whatever is commendable—if there is any moral excellence and if there is any praise—dwell on these things.

Philippians 4:7-8 HCSB

Genuine Peace

Sometimes, peace can be a scarce commodity in a demanding, 21st-century world. How, then, can we find the peace that we so desperately desire? By turning our days and our lives over to God.

The Scottish preacher George McDonald observed, "It has been well said that no man ever sank under the burden of the day. It is when tomorrow's burden is added to the burden of today that the weight is more than a man can bear. Never load yourselves so, my friends. If you find yourselves so loaded, at least remember this: it is your own doing, not God's. He begs you to leave the future to Him."

May we give our lives, our hopes, our prayers, and our futures to the Father, and, by doing so, accept His will and His peace.

More Great Ideas About Peace

When you and I are related to Jesus Christ, our strength and wisdom and peace and joy and love and hope may run out, but His life rushes in to keep us filled to the brim. We are showered with blessings, not because of anything we have or have not done, but simply because of Him.

Anne Graham Lotz

We're prone to want God to change our circumstances, but He wants to change our character. We think that peace comes from the outside in, but it comes from the inside out.

Warren Wiersbe

Peace is the deepest thing a human personality can know; it is almighty.

Oswald Chambers

God's peace is like a river, not a pond. In other words, a sense of health and well-being, both of which are expressions of the Hebrew *shalom*, can permeate our homes even when we're in white-water rapids.

Beth Moore

That peace, which has been described and which believers enjoy, is a participation of the peace which their glorious Lord and Master himself enjoys.

Jonathan Edwards

Thou hast formed us for Thyself, and our hearts are restless till they find rest in Thee.

St. Augustine

What peace can they have who are not at peace with God?

Matthew Henry

God has promised us abundance, peace, and eternal life. These treasures are ours for the asking; all we must do is claim them. One of the great mysteries of life is why on earth do so many of us wait so very long to claim them?

Marie T. Freeman

God is in control of history; it's His story. Doesn't that give you a great peace—especially when world events seem so tumultuous and insane?

Kay Arthur

Do you not know that the runners in a stadium all race,
but only one receives the prize? Run in such a way that you
may win. Now everyone who competes exercises self-control
in everything. However, they do it to receive a perishable
crown, but we an imperishable one.

1 Corinthians 9:24-25 HCSB

The Power of Perseverance

In a world filled with roadblocks and stumbling blocks, we need strength, courage, and perseverance. And, as an example of perfect perseverance, we need look no further than our Savior, Jesus Christ.

Jesus finished what He began. Despite the torture He endured, despite the shame of the cross, Jesus was steadfast in His faithfulness to God. We, too, must remain faithful, especially during times of hardship.

Perhaps you are in a hurry for God to reveal His plans for your life. If so, be forewarned: God operates on His own timetable, not yours. Sometimes, God may answer your prayers with silence, and when He does, you must patiently persevere. In times of trouble, you must remain steadfast and trust in the merciful goodness of your Heavenly Father. Whatever your problem, He can handle it.

More Great Ideas About Perseverance

You cannot persevere unless there is a trial in your life. There can be no victories without battles; there can be no peaks without valleys. If you want the blessing, you must be prepared to carry the burden and fight the battle. God has to balance privileges with responsibilities, blessings with burdens, or else you and I will become spoiled, pampered children.

Warren Wiersbe

Perseverance is more than endurance. It is endurance combined with absolute assurance and certainty that what we are looking for is going to happen.

Oswald Chambers

Only the man who follows the command of Jesus single-mindedly and unresistingly lets his yoke rest upon him, finds his burden easy, and under its gentle pressure receives the power to persevere in the right way.

Dietrich Bonhoeffer

By perseverance the snail reached the ark.

C. H. Spurgeon

Battles are won in the trenches, in the grit and grime of courageous determination; they are won day by day in the arena of life.

Charles Swindoll

We are all on our way somewhere. We'll get there if we just keep going.

Barbara Johnson

If things are tough, remember that every flower that ever bloomed had to go through a whole lot of dirt to get there.

Barbara Johnson

Failure is one of life's most powerful teachers. How we handle our failures determines whether we're going to simply "get by" in life or "press on."

Beth Moore

Are you a Christian? If you are, how can you be hopeless? Are you so depressed by the greatness of your problems that you have given up all hope? Instead of giving up, would you patiently endure? Would you focus on Christ until you are so preoccupied with him alone that you fall prostrate before him?

Anne Graham Lotz

Honor His holy name; let the hearts of those who seek the Lord rejoice. Search for the Lord and for His strength; seek His face always.

1 Chronicles 16:10-11 HCSB

Seeking God

Sometimes, in the crush of our daily duties, God may seem far away, but He is not. God is everywhere we have ever been and everywhere we will ever go. He is with us night and day; He knows our thoughts and our prayers. And, when we earnestly seek Him, we will find Him because He is here, waiting patiently for us to reach out to Him.

If you have been touched by the transforming love of Jesus, then you have every reason to live courageously. After all, Christ has already won the ultimate battle—and He won it for you—on the cross at Calvary. Still, even if you are a dedicated Christian, you may find yourself discouraged by the inevitable disappointments and tragedies that occur in the lives of believers and non-believers alike.

The next time you find your courage tested to the limit, lean upon God's promises. Trust His Son. Remember that God is always near and that He is your protector and your deliverer. And please remember that no matter your circumstances, God will never leave you. He is always present, always loving, always ready to comfort and protect.

More Great Ideas About Seeking God

Thirsty hearts are those whose longings have been wakened by the touch of God within them.

A. W. Tozer

But I'm convinced the best way to cope with change, ironically enough, is to get to know a God who doesn't change, One who provides an anchor in the swirling seas of change.

Bill Hybels

Don't take anyone else's word for God. Find him for yourself, and then you, too, will know, by the wonderful, warm tug on your heartstrings, that he is there for sure.

Billy Graham

You can see the world by standing tall, but to witness the Savior, you have to get on your knees.

Max Lucado

For am I now trying to win the favor of people, or God? Or am I striving to please people? If I were still trying to please people, I would not be a slave of Christ.

Galatians 1:10 HCSB

Choosing to Please God

Whom will you try to please today: God or man? Your primary obligation is not to please imperfect men and women. Your obligation is to strive diligently to meet the expectations of an all-knowing and perfect God.

Sometimes, because you're an imperfect human being, you may become so wrapped up in meeting society's expectations that you fail to focus on God's expectations. To do so is a mistake of major proportions—don't make it. Instead, seek God's guidance as you focus your energies on becoming the best "you" that you can possibly be. And, when it comes to matters of conscience, seek approval not from your peers, but from your Creator.

More Great Ideas About Pleasing God

All our offerings, whether music or martyrdom, are like the intrinsically worthless present of a child, which a father values indeed, but values only for the intention.

C. S. Lewis

It is impossible to please God doing things motivated by and produced by the flesh.

Bill Bright

It is impossible to please everybody. It's not impossible to please God. So try pleasing God.

Jim Gallery

You must never sacrifice your relationship with God for the sake of a relationship with another person.

Charles Stanley

Faithfulness today is the best preparation for the demands of tomorrow.

Elisabeth Elliot

A heart out of tune,
out of sync with God's heart,
will produce a life of spiritual
barrenness and missed
opportunities.

—

Jim Cymbala

Thanks be to God for His indescribable gift.

2 Corinthians 9:15 HCSB

A Thankful Heart

Sometimes, life here on earth can be complicated, demanding, and frustrating. When the demands of life leave us rushing from place to place with scarcely a moment to spare, we may fail to pause and thank our Creator for the countless blessings He bestows upon us. But, whenever we neglect to give proper thanks to the Giver of all things good, we suffer because of our misplaced priorities.

As believers who have been saved by a risen Christ, we are blessed beyond human comprehension. We who have been given so much should make thanksgiving a habit, a regular part of our daily routines. Of course, God's gifts are too numerous to count, but we should attempt to count them nonetheless. We owe our Heavenly Father everything, including our eternal praise . . . starting right now.

More Great Ideas About Thanksgiving

God often keeps us on the path by guiding us through the counsel of friends and trusted spiritual advisors.

Bill Hybels

The act of thanksgiving is a demonstration of the fact that you are going to trust and believe God.

Kay Arthur

If you won't fill your heart with gratitude, the devil will fill it with something else.

Marie T. Freeman

The words "thank" and "think" come from the same root word. If we would think more, we would thank more.

Warren Wiersbe

It is always possible to be thankful for what is given rather than to complain about what is not given. One or the other becomes a habit of life.

Elisabeth Elliot

God has promised that
if we harvest well with the tools
of thanksgiving, there will be
seeds for planting in the spring.

—

Gloria Gaither

Therefore, as we have opportunity, we must work for the good of all, especially for those who belong to the household of faith.

Galatians 6:10 HCSB

Today's Opportunities

Are you excited about the opportunities of today and thrilled by the possibilities of tomorrow? Do you confidently expect God to lead you to a place of abundance, peace, and joy? And, when your days on earth are over, do you expect to receive the priceless gift of eternal life? If you trust God's promises, and if you have welcomed God's Son into your heart, then you believe that your future is intensely and eternally bright.

Today, as you prepare to meet the duties of everyday life, pause and consider God's promises. And then think for a moment about the wonderful future that awaits all believers, including you. God has promised that your future is secure. Trust that promise, and celebrate the life of abundance and eternal joy that is now yours through Christ.

More Great Ideas About Opportunities

He who waits until circumstances completely favor his undertaking will never accomplish anything.

Martin Luther

God surrounds you with opportunity. You and I are free in Jesus Christ, not to do whatever we want, but to be all that God wants us to be.

Warren Wiersbe

We are all faced with a series of great opportunities, brilliantly disguised as unsolvable problems. Unsolvable without God's wisdom, that is.

Charles Swindoll

Great opportunities often disguise themselves in small tasks.

Rick Warren

Winners see an answer for every problem; losers see a problem in every answer.

Barbara Johnson

Life is a glorious opportunity.

—

Billy Graham

In the beginning God created the heavens and the earth. The earth was without form, and void; and darkness was on the face of the deep. And the Spirit of God was hovering over the face of the waters. Then God said, "Let there be light"; and there was light.

Genesis 1:1-3 NKJV

Celebrating God's Creation

In the beginning, God created everything: the things we see and the things we don't. And each morning, the sun rises upon a glorious world that is a physical manifestation of God's infinite power and His infinite love. And yet, because of the incessant demands of everyday life, we're sometimes too busy to notice.

We live in a society filled with more distractions than we can possibly count and more obligations than we can possibly meet. Is it any wonder, then, that we often overlook God's handiwork as we rush from place to place, giving scarcely a single thought to the beauty that surrounds us?

Today, take time to really observe the world around you. Take time to offer a prayer of thanks for the sky above and the beauty that lies beneath it. And take time to ponder the miracle of God's creation. The time you spend celebrating God's wonderful world is always time well spent.

More Great Ideas About God's Creation

No philosophical theory which I have yet come across is a radical improvement on the words of Genesis, that "in the beginning God made Heaven and Earth."

C. S. Lewis

Man was created by God to know and love Him in a permanent, personal relationship.

Anne Graham Lotz

God expresses His love through creation.

Charles Stanley

How awesome that the "Word" that was in the beginning, by which and through which God created everything, was—and is—a living Person with a mind, will, emotions, and intellect.

Anne Graham Lotz

I am the vine, you are the branches. He who abides in Me, and I in him, bears much fruit; for without Me you can do nothing.

John 15:5 NKJV

He Is the Vine

He was the Son of God, but He wore a crown of thorns. He was the Savior of mankind, yet He was put to death on a roughhewn cross. He offered His healing touch to an unsaved world, and yet the same hands that had healed the sick and raised the dead were pierced with nails.

Jesus Christ, the Son of God, was born into humble circumstances. He walked this earth, not as a ruler of men, but as the Savior of mankind. His crucifixion, a torturous punishment that was intended to end His life and His reign, instead became the pivotal event in the history of all humanity. Christ sacrificed His life on the cross so that we might have eternal life. This gift, freely given by God's only begotten Son, is the priceless possession of everyone who accepts Him as Lord and Savior.

Why did Christ endure the humiliation and torture of the cross? He did it for you. His love is as near as your next breath, as personal as your next thought, more essential than your next heartbeat. And what must you do in response to the Savior's gifts? You must accept His love, praise His name, and share His message of salvation. And, you must conduct yourself in a manner that demonstrates to all the world that your acquaintance with the Master is not a passing fancy but that it is, instead, the cornerstone and the touchstone of your life.

When you can't see him,
trust him.
Jesus is closer than you
ever dreamed.

—

Max Lucado

More Great Ideas About Jesus

Tell me the story of Jesus. Write on my heart every word. Tell me the story most precious, sweetest that ever was heard.

Fanny Crosby

Had Jesus been the Word become word, He would have spun theories about life, but since he was the Word become flesh, he put shoes on all his theories and made them walk.

E. Stanley Jones

Jesus was the perfect reflection of God's nature in every situation He encountered during His time here on earth.

Bill Hybels

Sold for thirty pieces of silver, he redeemed the world.

R. G. Lee

There is not a single thing that Jesus cannot change, control, and conquer because He is the living Lord.

Franklin Graham

*Ask, and it will be given to you; seek, and you will find;
knock, and it will be opened to you. For everyone who asks
receives, and he who seeks finds, and to him who knocks it
will be opened.*

Matthew 7:7-8 NKJV

Ask Him for the Things You Need

How often do you ask God for His help and His wisdom? Occasionally? Intermittently? Whenever you experience a crisis? Hopefully not. Hopefully, you've acquired the habit of asking for God's assistance early and often. And hopefully, you have learned to seek His guidance in every aspect of your life.

In Matthew 7, God promises that He will guide you if you let Him. Your job is to let Him. But sometimes, you will be tempted to do otherwise. Sometimes, you'll be tempted to go along with the crowd; other times, you'll be tempted to do things your way, not God's way. When you feel those temptations, resist them.

God has promised that when you ask for His help, He will not withhold it. So ask. Ask Him to meet the needs of your day. Ask Him to lead you, to protect you, and to correct you. And trust the answers He gives.

God stands at the door and waits. When you knock, He opens. When you ask, He answers. Your task, of course, is to seek His guidance prayerfully, confidently, and often.

More Great Ideas About Asking God

By asking in Jesus' name, we're making a request not only in His authority, but also for His interests and His benefit.

Shirley Dobson

Some people think God does not like to be troubled with our constant asking. But, the way to trouble God is not to come at all.

D. L. Moody

All we have to do is to acknowledge our need, move from self-sufficiency to dependence, and ask God to become our hiding place.

Bill Hybels

God's help is always available, but it is only given to those who seek it.

Max Lucado

God uses our most stumbling, faltering faith-steps as the open door to His doing for us "more than we ask or think."

Catherine Marshall

Often I have made a request of God with earnest pleadings even backed up with Scripture, only to have Him say "No" because He had something better in store.

Ruth Bell Graham

Notice that we must ask. And we will sometimes struggle to hear and struggle with what we hear. But personally, it's worth it. I'm after the path of life—and he alone knows it.

John Eldredge

God makes prayer as easy as possible for us. He's completely approachable and available, and He'll never mock or upbraid us for bringing our needs before Him.

Shirley Dobson

Don't be afraid to ask your heavenly Father for anything you need. Indeed, nothing is too small for God's attention or too great for his power.

Dennis Swanberg

You shall have no other gods before Me.

Exodus 20:3 NKJV

Putting God First

I s God your top priority? Have you given His Son your heart, your soul, your talents, and your time? Or are you in the habit of giving God little more than a few hours on Sunday morning? The answers to these questions will determine how you prioritize your days and your life.

As you contemplate your own relationship with God, remember this: all of mankind is engaged in the practice of worship. Some people choose to worship God and, as a result, reap the joy that He intends for His children. Others distance themselves from God by worshiping such things as earthly possessions or personal gratification . . . and when they do so, they suffer.

In the book of Exodus, God warns that we should place no gods before Him. Yet all too often, we place our Lord in second, third, or fourth place as we worship the gods of pride, greed, power, or lust.

When we place our desires for material possessions above our love for God—or when we yield to temptations of the flesh—we find ourselves engaged in a struggle that is similar to the one Jesus faced when He was tempted by Satan. In the wilderness, Satan offered Jesus earthly power and unimaginable riches, but Jesus turned Satan away and chose instead to worship God. We must do likewise by putting God first and worshiping only Him.

Does God rule your heart? Make certain that the honest answer to this question is a resounding yes. In the life of every righteous believer, God comes first. That's precisely the place that He deserves in your heart, too.

You must never sacrifice your relationship with God for the sake of a relationship with another person.

—

Charles Stanley

More Great Ideas About Putting God First

Make God's will the focus of your life day by day. If you seek to please Him and Him alone, you'll find yourself satisfied with life.

Kay Arthur

It is impossible to please God doing things motivated by and produced by the flesh.

Bill Bright

A man's spiritual health is exactly proportional to his love for God.

C. S. Lewis

I love you, Lord, not doubtingly, but with absolute certainty. Your Word beat upon my heart until I fell in love with you, and now the universe and everything in it tells me to love you, and tells the same thing to us all.

St. Augustine

Jesus Christ is the first and last, author and finisher, beginning and end, alpha and omega, and by Him all other things hold together. He must be first or nothing. God never comes next!

Vance Havner

I am come that they might have life, and that they might have it more abundantly.

John 10:10 KJV

Accepting God's Abundance

The 10th chapter of John tells us that Christ came to earth so that our lives might be filled with abundance. But what, exactly, did Jesus mean when He promised "life…more abundantly"? Was He referring to material possessions or financial wealth? Hardly. Jesus offers a different kind of abundance: a spiritual richness that extends beyond the temporal boundaries of this world.

Is material abundance part of God's plan for our lives? Perhaps. But in every circumstance of life, during times of wealth or times of want, God will provide us what we need if we trust Him (Matthew 6). May we, as believers, claim the riches of Christ Jesus every day that we live, and may we share His blessings with all who cross our path.

More Great Ideas About Abundance

The gift of God is eternal life, spiritual life, abundant life through faith in Jesus Christ, the Living Word of God.

Anne Graham Lotz

God's riches are beyond anything we could ask or even dare to imagine! If my life gets gooey and stale, I have no excuse.

Barbara Johnson

The only way you can experience abundant life is to surrender your plans to Him.

Charles Stanley

God loves you and wants you to experience peace and life—abundant and eternal.

Billy Graham

The Bible says that being a Christian is not only a great way to die, but it's also the best way to live.

Bill Hybels

After this manner therefore pray ye: Our Father which art in heaven, Hallowed be thy name. Thy kingdom come. Thy will be done in earth, as it is in heaven. Give us this day our daily bread. And forgive us our debts, as we forgive our debtors. And lead us not into temptation, but deliver us from evil: For thine is the kingdom, and the power, and the glory, for ever. Amen

Matthew 6:9-13 KJV

The Lord's Prayer

"Our Father which art in heaven, hallowed be thy name." These familiar words begin the Lord's Prayer, a prayer that you've heard on countless occasions. It's the prayer that Jesus taught His followers to pray, and it's a prayer that you probably know by heart.

You already know what the prayer says, but have you thought carefully, and in detail, about exactly what those words mean? Hopefully so. After all, this simple prayer was authored by the Savior of mankind.

Today, take the time to carefully consider each word in this beautiful passage. When you weave the Lord's Prayer into the fabric of your life, you'll soon discover that God's Word and God's Son have the power to change everything, including you.

More Great Ideas About God

I lived with Indians who made pots out of clay which they used for cooking. Nobody was interested in the pot. Everybody was interested in what was inside. The same clay taken out of the same riverbed, always made in the same design, nothing special about it. Well, I'm a clay pot, and let me not forget it. But, the excellency of the power is of God and not us.

Elisabeth Elliot

God is the beyond in the midst of our life.

Dietrich Bonhoeffer

The God who dwells in heaven is willing to dwell also in the heart of the humble believer.

Warren Wiersbe

God is not a supernatural interferer; God is the everlasting portion of his people. When a man born from above begins his new life, he meets God at every turn, hears him in every sound, sleeps at his feet, and wakes to find him there.

Oswald Chambers

God is an infinite circle
whose center is everywhere
and whose circumference
is nowhere.

—

St. Augustine

The Lord is my shepherd; I shall not want. He makes me to lie down in green pastures; He leads me beside the still waters. He restores my soul.

Psalm 23:1-3 NKJV

God's Protection

David, the author of the 23rd Psalm, realized that God was his shield, his protector, and his salvation. And if we're wise, we realize it, too. After all, God has promised to protect us, and He intends to keep His promise.

In a world filled with dangers and temptations, God is the ultimate armor. In a world filled with misleading messages, God's Word is the ultimate truth. In a world filled with more frustrations than we can count, God's Son offers the ultimate peace.

Will you accept God's peace and wear God's armor against the dangers of our world? Hopefully so—because when you do, you can live courageously, knowing that you possess the supreme protection: God's unfailing love for you.

The world offers no safety nets, but God does. He sent His only begotten Son to offer you the priceless gift of eternal life. And now you are challenged to return

God's love by obeying His commandments and honoring His Son.

Sometimes, in the crush of everyday life, God may seem far away, but He is not. God is everywhere you have ever been and everywhere you will ever go. He is with you night and day; He knows your thoughts and your prayers. And, when you earnestly seek His protection, you will find it because He is here—always—waiting patiently for you to reach out to Him. And the next move, of course, is yours.

Prayer is our pathway
not only to divine protection,
but also to a personal, intimate
relationship with God.

—

Shirley Dobson

More Great Ideas About God's Protection

He goes before us, follows behind us, and hems us safe inside the realm of His protection.

Beth Moore

The Lord God of heaven and earth, the Almighty Creator of all things, He who holds the universe in His hand as though it were a very little thing, He is your Shepherd, and He has charged Himself with the care and keeping of you, as a shepherd is charged with the care and keeping of his sheep.

Hannah Whitall Smith

Kept by His power—that is the only safety.

Oswald Chambers

Our responsibility is to feed from Him, to stay close to Him, to follow Him—because sheep easily go astray—so that we eternally experience the protection and companionship of our Great Shepherd the Lord Jesus Christ.

Franklin Graham

Therefore, whatever you want others to do for you, do also the same for them—this is the Law and the Prophets.

Matthew 7:12 HCSB

The Golden Rule

The words of Matthew 7:12 remind us that, as believers in Christ, we are commanded to treat others as we wish to be treated. This commandment is, indeed, the Golden Rule for Christians of every generation. When we weave the thread of kindness into the very fabric of our lives, we give glory to the One who gave His life for ours.

Because we are imperfect human beings, we are, on occasion, selfish, thoughtless, or cruel. But God commands us to behave otherwise. He teaches us to rise above our own imperfections and to treat others with unselfishness and love. When we observe God's Golden Rule, we help build His kingdom here on earth. And, when we share the love of Christ, we share a priceless gift; may we share it today and every day that we live.

More Great Ideas About the Golden Rule

It is one of the most beautiful compensations of life that no one can sincerely try to help another without helping herself.

Barbara Johnson

The Golden Rule starts at home, but it should never stop there.

Marie T. Freeman

The golden rule to follow to obtain spiritual understanding is not one of intellectual pursuit, but one of obedience.

Oswald Chambers

When you extend hospitality to others, you're not trying to impress people, you're trying to reflect God to them.

Max Lucado

Be so preoccupied with good will that you haven't room for ill will.

E. Stanley Jones

Choices can change our lives profoundly. The choice to mend a broken relationship, to say "yes" to a difficult assignment, to lay aside some important work to play with a child, to visit some forgotten person—these small choices may affect many lives eternally.

Gloria Gaither

Your light is the truth of the Gospel message itself as well as your witness as to Who Jesus is and what He has done for you. Don't hide it.

Anne Graham Lotz

In your desire to share the gospel, you may be the only Jesus someone else will ever meet. Be real and be involved with people.

Barbara Johnson

Love is not grabbing, or self-centered, or selfish. Real love is being able to contribute to the happiness of another person without expecting to get anything in return.

James Dobson

Commit your activities to the Lord and your plans will be achieved.

Proverbs 16:3 HCSB

Defining Success

How do you define success? Do you define it as the accumulation of material possessions or the adulation of your neighbors? If so, you need to reorder your priorities. Genuine success has little to do with fame or fortune; it has everything to do with God's gift of love and His promise of salvation.

If you have accepted Christ as your personal Savior, you are already a towering success in the eyes of God, but there is still more that you can do. Your task—as a believer who has been touched by the Creator's grace—is to accept the spiritual abundance and peace that He offers through the person of His Son. Then, you can share the healing message of God's love and His abundance with a world that desperately needs both. When you do, you will have reached the pinnacle of success.

More Great Ideas About Success

Winners see an answer for every problem; losers see a problem in every answer.

Barbara Johnson

In essence, my testimony is that there is life after failure: abundant, effective, spirit-filled life for those who are willing to repent hard and work hard.

Beth Moore

There's not much you can't achieve or endure if you know God is walking by your side. Just remember: Someone knows, and Someone cares.

Bill Hybels

We, as believers, must allow God to define success. And, when we do, God blesses us with His love and His grace.

Jim Gallery

Success or failure can be pretty well predicted by the degree to which the heart is fully in it.

John Eldredge

God provides the ingredients for our daily bread but expects us to do the baking. With our own hands!

Barbara Johnson

Maintenance of the devotional mood is indispensable to success in the Christian life.

A. W. Tozer

Often, attitude is the only difference between success and failure.

John Maxwell

Success isn't the key. Faithfulness is.

Joni Eareckson Tada

Victory is the result of Christ's life lived out in the believer. It is important to see that victory, not defeat, is God's purpose for His children.

Corrie ten Boom

Success and happiness are not destinations. They are exciting, never-ending journeys.

Zig Ziglar

The one who conceals his sins will not prosper, but whoever confesses and renounces them will find mercy.

Proverbs 28:13 HCSB

When You Make a Mistake

Everybody makes mistakes, and so will you. In fact, Winston Churchill once observed, "Success is going from failure to failure without loss of enthusiasm." What was good for Churchill is also good for you. You should expect to make mistakes—plenty of mistakes—but you should not allow those missteps to rob you of the enthusiasm you need to fulfill God's plan for your life.

We are imperfect people living in an imperfect world; mistakes are simply part of the price we pay for being here. But, even though mistakes are an inevitable part of life's journey, repeated mistakes should not be. When we commit the inevitable blunders of life, we must correct them, learn from them, and pray for the wisdom not to repeat them. When we do, our mistakes become lessons, and our lives become adventures in growth, not stagnation.

Have you made a mistake or three? Of course you have. But here's the big question: have you used your mistakes as stumbling blocks or stepping stones? The answer to that question will determine how well you will perform in the workplace and in every other aspect of your life.

Mistakes offer the possibility for redemption and a new start in God's kingdom. No matter what you're guilty of, God can restore your innocence.

—

Barbara Johnson

More Great Ideas About Mistakes

God is able to take mistakes, when they are committed to Him, and make of them something for our good and for His glory.

Ruth Bell Graham

One of the ways God refills us after failure is through the blessing of Christian fellowship. Just experiencing the joy of simple activities shared with other children of God can have a healing effect on us.

Anne Graham Lotz

In essence, my testimony is that there is life after failure: abundant, effective, spirit-filled life for those who are willing to repent hard and work hard.

Beth Moore

Sin is largely a matter of mistaken priorities. Any sin in us that is cherished, hidden, and not confessed will cut the nerve center of our faith.

Catherine Marshall

Truth will sooner come out of error than from confusion.

Francis Bacon

Be still, and know that I am God….

Psalm 46:10 KJV

Be Still

We live in a noisy world, a world filled with distractions, frustrations, obligations, and complications. But we must not allow our clamorous world to separate us from God's peace. Instead, we must "be still" so that we might sense the presence of God.

If we are to maintain righteous minds and compassionate hearts, we must take time each day for prayer and for meditation. We must make ourselves still in the presence of our Creator. We must quiet our minds and our hearts so that we might sense God's love, God's will, and God's Son.

Has the busy pace of life robbed you of the peace that might otherwise be yours through Jesus Christ? If so, it's time to reorder your priorities. Nothing is more important than the time you spend with your Savior. So be still and claim the inner peace that is your spiritual birthright: the peace of Jesus Christ. It is offered freely; it has been paid for in full; it is yours for the asking. So ask. And then share.

More Great Ideas About Quiet Time

The manifold rewards of a serious, consistent prayer life demonstrate clearly that time with our Lord should be our first priority.

Shirley Dobson

I don't see how any Christian can survive, let alone live life as more than a conqueror, apart from a quiet time alone with God.

Kay Arthur

When we are in the presence of God, removed from distractions, we are able to hear him more clearly, and a secure environment has been established for the young and broken places in our hearts to surface.

John Eldredge

The Lord Jesus, available to people much of the time, left them, sometimes a great while before day, to go up to the hills where He could commune in solitude with His Father.

Elisabeth Elliot

Since the quiet hour spent with God is the preacher's power-house, the devil centers his attention on that source of strength.

Vance Havner

Quiet time is giving God your undivided attention for a predetermined amount of time for the purpose of talking to and hearing from Him.

Charles Stanley

Let this be your chief object in prayer, to realize the presence of your heavenly Father. Let your watchword be: Alone with God.

Andrew Murray

In the center of a hurricane there is absolute quiet and peace. There is no safer place than in the center of the will of God.

Corrie ten Boom

When frustrations develop into problems that stress you out, the best way to cope is to stop, catch your breath, and do something for yourself, not out of selfishness, but out of wisdom.

Barbara Johnson

And now abide faith, hope, love, these three; but the greatest of these is love.

1 Corinthians 13:13 NKJV

The Greatest of These Is Love

The familiar words of 1st Corinthians 13 remind us of the importance of love. Faith is important, of course. So too is hope. But love is more important still.

Christ showed His love for us on the cross, and, as Christians, we are called upon to return Christ's love by sharing it. We are commanded (not advised, not encouraged…commanded!) to love one another just as Christ loved us (John 13:34). That's a tall order, but as Christians, we are obligated to follow it.

Sometimes love is easy (puppies and sleeping children come to mind) and sometimes love is hard (fallible human beings come to mind). But God's Word is clear: We are to love our all our friends and neighbors, not just the lovable ones. So today, take time to spread Christ's message by word and by example. And the greatest of these is, of course, is example.

More Great Ideas About Love

Those who abandon ship the first time it enters a storm miss the calm beyond. And the rougher the storms weathered together, the deeper and stronger real love grows.

Ruth Bell Graham

Love is an attribute of God. To love others is evidence of a genuine faith.

Kay Arthur

How much a person loves someone is obvious by how much he is willing to sacrifice for that person.

Bill Bright

He who is filled with love is filled with God Himself.

St. Augustine

Live your lives in love, the same sort of love which Christ gives us, and which He perfectly expressed when He gave Himself as a sacrifice to God.

Corrie ten Boom

How do you spell love? When you reach the point where the happiness, security, and development of another person is as much of a driving force to you as your own happiness, security, and development, then you have a mature love. True love is spelled G-I-V-E. It is not based on what you can get, but rooted in what you can give to the other person.

Josh McDowell

Love is the seed of all hope. It is the enticement to trust, to risk, to try, and to go on.

Gloria Gaither

It is when we come to the Lord in our nothingness, our powerlessness and our helplessness that He then enables us to love in a way which, without Him, would be absolutely impossible.

Elisabeth Elliot

Suppose that I understand the Bible. And, suppose that I am the greatest preacher who ever lived! The Apostle Paul wrote that unless I have love, "I am nothing."

Billy Graham

But seek first the kingdom of God and His righteousness, and all these things shall be added to you. Therefore do not worry about tomorrow, for tomorrow will worry about its own things. Sufficient for the day is its own trouble.

Matthew 6:33-34 NKJV

Beyond Worry

Because we are imperfect human beings struggling with imperfect circumstances, we worry. Even though we, as Christians, have the assurance of salvation—even though we, as Christians, have the promise of God's love and protection—we find ourselves fretting over the inevitable frustrations of everyday life. Jesus understood our concerns when He spoke the reassuring words found in the 6th chapter of Matthew.

Where is the best place to take your worries? Take them to God. Take your troubles to Him; take your fears to Him; take your doubts to Him; take your weaknesses to Him; take your sorrows to Him . . . and leave them all there. Seek protection from the One who offers you eternal salvation; build your spiritual house upon the Rock that cannot be moved.

Perhaps you are concerned about your future, your health, or your finances. Or perhaps you are simply a "worrier" by nature. If so, make Matthew 6 a regular part of your daily Bible reading. This beautiful passage will remind you that God still sits in His heaven and you are His beloved child. Then, perhaps, you will worry a little less and trust God a little more, and that's as it should be because God is trustworthy . . . and you are protected.

Today is the tomorrow we worried about yesterday.

Dennis Swanberg

More Great Ideas About Worry

Worry is the senseless process of cluttering up tomorrow's opportunities with leftover problems from today.

Barbara Johnson

Never yield to gloomy anticipation. Place your hope and confidence in God. He has no record of failure.

Mrs. Charles E. Cowman

God is bigger than your problems. Whatever worries press upon you today, put them in God's hands and leave them there.

Billy Graham

The beginning of anxiety is the end of faith, and the beginning of true faith is the end of anxiety.

George Mueller

Much that worries us beforehand can, quite unexpectedly, have a happy and simple solution. Worries just don't matter. Things really are in a better hand than ours.

Dietrich Bonhoeffer

We are not called to be burden-bearers, but cross-bearers and light-bearers. We must cast our burdens on the Lord.

Corrie ten Boom

Trust in the Lord with all your heart, and lean not on your own understanding; in all your ways acknowledge Him, and He shall direct your paths.

Proverbs 3:5-6 NKJV

Trust Him

I t's easy to talk about trusting God, but when it comes to actually trusting Him, that's considerably harder. Why? Because genuine trust in God requires more than words; it requires a willingness to follow God's lead and a willingness to obey His commandments.

Have you spent more time talking about Christ than walking in His footsteps? If so, God wants to have a little chat with you. And, if you're unwilling to talk to Him, He may take other actions in order to grab your attention.

Thankfully, whenever you're willing to talk with God, He's willing to listen. And, the instant that you decide to place Him squarely in the center of your life, He will respond to that decision with blessings that are too unexpected to predict and too numerous to count.

When you find your courage tested to the limit, lean upon God's promises. Trust His Son. Remember that God is always near and that He is your protector and your deliverer. When you are worried, anxious, or afraid, call upon Him. God can handle your troubles infinitely better than you can, so turn them over to Him. Remember that God rules both mountaintops and valleys—with limitless wisdom and love—now and forever.

God is God.
He knows what he is doing.
When you can't trace his hand,
trust his heart.

—

Max Lucado

More Great Ideas About Trusting God

Sometimes the very essence of faith is trusting God in the midst of things He knows good and well we cannot comprehend.

Beth Moore

A prayerful heart and an obedient heart will learn, very slowly and not without sorrow, to stake everything on God Himself.

Elisabeth Elliot

Faith does not eliminate problems. Faith keeps you in a trusting relationship with God in the midst of your problems.

Henry Blackaby

Do not be afraid, then, that if you trust, or tell others to trust, the matter will end there. Trust is only the beginning and the continual foundation. When we trust Him, the Lord works, and His work is the important part of the whole matter.

Hannah Whitall Smith

Guard your heart above all else, for it is the source of life.

Proverbs 4:23 HCSB

Guard Your Heart

You are near and dear to God. He loves you more than you can imagine, and He wants the very best for you. And one more thing: God wants you to guard your heart.

Every day, you are faced with choices . . . more choices than you can count. You can do the right thing, or not. You can be prudent, or not. You can be kind, and generous, and obedient to God. Or not.

Today, the world will offer you countless opportunities to let down your guard and, by doing so, make needless mistakes that may injure you or your loved ones. So be watchful and obedient. Guard your heart by giving it to your Heavenly Father; it is safe with Him.

More Great Ideas About Guarding Your Heart

We can't stop the Adversary from whispering in our ears, but we can refuse to listen, and we can definitely refuse to respond.

Liz Curtis Higgs

Our actions are seen by people, but our motives are monitored by God.

Franklin Graham

A man's poverty before God is judged by the disposition of his heart, not by his coffers.

St. Augustine

The more wisdom enters our hearts, the more we will be able to trust our hearts in difficult situations.

John Eldredge

The God who dwells in heaven is willing to dwell also in the heart of the humble believer.

Warren Wiersbe

Then He said to them all, "If anyone desires to come after Me, let him deny himself, and take up his cross daily, and follow Me. For whoever desires to save his life will lose it, but whoever loses his life for My sake will save it."

Luke 9:23-24 NKJV

Follow Him

Jesus walks with you. Are you walking with Him? Hopefully, you will choose to walk with Him today and every day of your life.

Jesus loved you so much that He endured unspeakable humiliation and suffering for you. How will you respond to Christ's sacrifice? Will you follow the instructions of Luke 9:23 by taking up His cross and following Him? Or will you choose another path? When you place your hopes squarely at the foot of the cross, when you place Jesus squarely at the center of your life, you will be blessed. If you seek to be a worthy disciple of Jesus, you must acknowledge that He never comes "next." He is always first.

Do you hope to fulfill God's purpose for your life? Do you seek a life of abundance and peace? Do you intend to be a Christian, not just in name, but in deed? Then follow Christ. Follow Him by picking up His cross today and every day that you live. When you do, you will quickly discover that Christ's love has the power to change everything, including you.

More Great Ideas About Following Jesus

As we live moment by moment under the control of the Spirit, His character, which is the character of Jesus, becomes evident to those around us.

Anne Graham Lotz

Peter said, "No, Lord!" But he had to learn that one cannot say "No" while saying "Lord" and that one cannot say "Lord" while saying "No."

Corrie ten Boom

A disciple is a follower of Christ. That means you take on His priorities as your own. His agenda becomes your agenda. His mission becomes your mission.

Charles Stanley

To walk out of His will is to walk into nowhere.

C. S. Lewis

The essence of the Christian life is Jesus: that in all things He might have the preeminence, not that in some things He might have a place.

Franklin Graham

Think of this—we may live together with Him here and now, a daily walking with Him who loved us and gave Himself for us.

Elisabeth Elliot

Will you, with a glad and eager surrender, hand yourself and all that concerns you over into his hands? If you will do this, your soul will begin to know something of the joy of union with Christ.

Hannah Whitall Smith

The Christian faith is meant to be lived moment by moment. It isn't some broad, general outline—it's a long walk with a real Person. Details count: passing thoughts, small sacrifices, a few encouraging words, little acts of kindness, brief victories over nagging sins.

Joni Eareckson Tada

Our battles are first won or lost in the secret places of our will in God's presence, never in full view of the world.

Oswald Chambers

As the Father loved Me, I also have loved you; abide in My love.

John 15:9 NKJV

Christ's Love

How much does Christ love us? More than we, as mere mortals, can comprehend. His love is perfect and steadfast. Even though we are fallible and wayward, the Good Shepherd cares for us still. Even though we have fallen far short of the Father's commandments, Christ loves us with a power and depth that are beyond our understanding. The sacrifice that Jesus made upon the cross was made for each of us, and His love endures to the edge of eternity and beyond.

Hannah Whitall Smith spoke to believers of every generation when she advised, "Keep your face upturned to Christ as the flowers do to the sun. Look, and your soul shall live and grow." How true. When we turn our hearts to Jesus, we receive His blessings, His peace, and His grace.

Christ is the ultimate Savior of mankind and the personal Savior of those who believe in Him. As His servants, we should place Him at the very center of our lives. And every day that God gives us breath, we should share Christ's love and His message with a world that needs both.

Christ's love changes everything. When you accept His gift of grace, you are transformed, not only for today, but also for all eternity. If you haven't already done so, accept Jesus Christ as your personal Savior. He's waiting patiently for you to invite Him into your heart. Please don't make Him wait a single minute longer.

The richest meaning of
your life is contained in the idea
that Christ loved you enough
to give His life for you.

—

Calvin Miller

More Great Ideas About Christ's Love

To God be the glory, great things He has done; / So loved He the world that He gave us His Son.

Fanny Crosby

Live your lives in love, the same sort of love which Christ gives us, and which He perfectly expressed when He gave Himself as a sacrifice to God.

Corrie ten Boom

No man ever loved like Jesus. He taught the blind to see and the dumb to speak. He died on the cross to save us. He bore our sins. And now God says, "Because He did, I can forgive you."

Billy Graham

This hard place in which you perhaps find yourself is the very place in which God is giving you opportunity to look only to Him, to spend time in prayer, and to learn long-suffering, gentleness, meekness—in short, to learn the depths of the love that Christ Himself has poured out on all of us.

Elisabeth Elliot

The greatest among you must be a servant. But those who exalt themselves will be humbled, and those who humble themselves will be exalted.

Matthew 23:11-12 NKJV

Staying Humble

As fallible human beings, we have so much to be humble about. Why, then, is humility such a difficult trait for us to master? Precisely because we are fallible human beings. Yet, if we are to grow and mature as Christians, we must strive to give credit where credit is due, starting, of course, with God and His only begotten Son.

As Christians, we have been refashioned and saved by Jesus Christ, and that salvation came not because of our own good works but because of God's grace. Thus, we are not "self-made"; we are "God-made" and we are "Christ-saved." How, then, can we be boastful? The answer, of course, is that, if we are honest with ourselves and with our God, we simply can't be boastful... we must, instead, be eternally grateful and exceedingly humble. Humility, however, is not easy for most of us. All too often, we are tempted to stick out our chests and say, "Look at me; look what I did!" But, in the quiet moments when we search the depths of our own hearts, we know better. Whatever "it" is, God did that. And He deserves the credit.

More Great Ideas About Humility

If you know who you are in Christ, your personal ego is not an issue.

Beth Moore

That's what I love about serving God. In His eyes, there are no little people . . . because there are no big people. We are all on the same playing field. We all start at square one. No one has it better than the other, or possesses unfair advantage.

Joni Eareckson Tada

Jesus had a humble heart. If He abides in us, pride will never dominate our lives.

Billy Graham

Humility is the fairest and rarest flower that blooms.

Charles Swindoll

Because Christ Jesus came to the world clothed in humility, he will always be found among those who are clothed with humility. He will be found among the humble people.

A. W. Tozer

I can usually sense that a leading is from the Holy Spirit when it calls me to humble myself, to serve somebody, to encourage somebody, or to give something away. Very rarely will the evil one lead us to do those kind of things.

Bill Hybels

We are never stronger than the moment we admit we are weak.

Beth Moore

That some of my hymns have been dictated by the blessed Holy Spirit I have no doubt; and that others have been the result of deep meditation I know to be true; but that the poet has any right to claim special merit for himself is certainly presumptuous.

Fanny Crosby

Faith itself cannot be strong where humility is weak.

C. H. Spurgeon

These things have I spoken unto you, that my joy might remain in you, and that your joy might be full.

John 15:11 KJV

Making His Joy, Your Joy

Christ made it clear: He intends that His joy should become our joy. Yet sometimes, amid the inevitable hustle and bustle of life here on earth, we can forfeit—albeit temporarily—the joy of Christ as we wrestle with the challenges of daily living.

Jonathan Edwards, the 18th-century American clergyman, observed, "Christ is not only a remedy for your weariness and trouble, but he will give you an abundance of the contrary: joy and delight. They who come to Christ do not only come to a resting-place after they have been wandering in a wilderness, but they come to a banqueting-house where they may rest, and where they may feast. They may cease from their former troubles and toils, and they may enter upon a course of delights and spiritual joys."

If, today, your heart is heavy, open the door of your soul to Christ. He will give you peace and joy. And, if you already have the joy of Christ in your heart, share it freely, just as Christ freely shared His joy with you.

More Great Ideas About Joy

If you can forgive the person you were, accept the person you are, and believe in the person you will become, you are headed for joy. So celebrate your life.

Barbara Johnson

The Christian lifestyle is not one of legalistic do's and don'ts, but one that is positive, attractive, and joyful.

Vonette Bright

Our sense of joy, satisfaction, and fulfillment in life increases, no matter what the circumstances, if we are in the center of God's will.

Billy Graham

Joy is the direct result of having God's perspective on our daily lives and the effect of loving our Lord enough to obey His commands and trust His promises.

Bill Bright

A life of intimacy with God is characterized by joy.

Oswald Chambers

Rejoice, the Lord is King; Your Lord and King adore!
Rejoice, give thanks and sing and triumph evermore.

Charles Wesley

Lord, I thank you for the promise of heaven and the
unexpected moments when you touch my heartstrings
with that longing for my eternal home.

Joni Eareckson Tada

God knows everything. He can manage everything, and
He loves us. Surely this is enough for a fullness of joy
that is beyond words.

Hannah Whitall Smith

God gives to us a heavenly gift called joy, radically
different in quality from any natural joy.

Elisabeth Elliot

Joy is the heart's harmonious response to the Lord's song
of love.

A. W. Tozer

For by grace you are saved through faith, and this is not from yourselves; it is God's gift—not from works, so that no one can boast.

Ephesians 2:8-9 HCSB

The Gift of Grace

In the second chapter of Ephesians, God promises that we will be saved by faith, not by works. It's no wonder, then, that someone once said that GRACE stands for God's Redemption At Christ's Expense. It's true—God sent His Son so that we might be redeemed from our sins. In doing so, our Heavenly Father demonstrated His infinite mercy and His infinite love. We have received countless gifts from God, but none can compare with the gift of salvation. God's grace is the ultimate gift, and we owe Him the ultimate in thanksgiving.

The gift of eternal life is the priceless possession of everyone who accepts God's Son as Lord and Savior. We return our Savior's love by welcoming Him into our hearts and sharing His message and His love. When we do so, we are blessed not only today but forever.

More Great Ideas About Grace

The Christian life is motivated, not by a list of do's and don'ts, but by the gracious outpouring of God's love and blessing.

Anne Graham Lotz

In the depths of our sin, Christ died for us. He did not wait for persons to get as close as possible through obedience to the law and righteous living.

Beth Moore

God's grand strategy, birthed in his grace toward us in Christ, and nurtured through the obedience of disciplined faith, is to release us into the redeemed life of our heart, knowing it will lead us back to him even as the North Star guides a ship across the vast unknown surface of the ocean.

John Eldredge

No one is beyond his grace. No situation, anywhere on earth, is too hard for God.

Jim Cymbala

Faith is a living, daring confidence in God's grace, so sure and certain that a man would stake his life on it a thousand times.

Martin Luther

The cross was heavy, the blood was real, and the price was extravagant. It would have bankrupted you or me, so he paid it for us. Call it simple. Call it a gift. But don't call it easy. Call it what it is. Call it grace.

Max Lucado

God shields us from most of the things we fear, but when He chooses not to shield us, He unfailingly allots grace in the measure needed.

Elisabeth Elliot

How beautiful it is to learn that grace isn't fragile, and that in the family of God we can fail and not be a failure.

Gloria Gaither

Grace is but glory begun, and glory is but grace perfected.

Jonathan Edwards

All Scripture is given by inspiration of God, and is profitable for doctrine, for reproof, for correction, for instruction in righteousness, that the man of God may be complete, thoroughly equipped for every good work.

2 Timothy 3:16-17 NKJV

The Use of Scripture

Is Bible study a high priority for you? The answer to this simple question will determine, to a surprising extent, the quality of your life and the direction of your faith.

As you establish priorities for life, you must decide whether God's Word will be a bright spotlight that guides your path every day or a tiny nightlight that occasionally flickers in the dark. The decision to study the Bible—or not—is yours and yours alone. But make no mistake: how you choose to use your Bible will have a profound impact on you and your loved ones.

George Mueller observed, "The vigor of our spiritual lives will be in exact proportion to the place held by the Bible in our lives and in our thoughts." In other words: the more you use your Bible, the more God will use you.

Perhaps you're one of those Christians who owns a bookshelf full of unread Bibles. If so, remember the old saying, "A Bible in the hand is worth two in the book-case." Or perhaps you're one of those folks who is simply "too busy" to find time for a daily dose of prayer and Bible study. If so, remember the old adage, "It's hard to stumble when you're on your knees."

God's Word can be a roadmap to a place of righteousness and abundance. Make it your roadmap. God's wisdom can be a light to guide your steps. Claim it as your light today, tomorrow, and every day of your life—and then walk confidently in the footsteps of God's Son.

The Bible is God's Word to man.

Kay Arthur

More Great Ideas About God's Word

The Holy Spirit is the Spirit of Truth, which means He always works according to and through the Word of God whether you feel Him or not.

Anne Graham Lotz

My meditation and study have shown me that, like God, His Word is holy, everlasting, absolutely true, powerful, personally fair, and never changing.

Bill Bright

Help me, Lord, to be a student of Your Word, that I might be a better servant in Your world.

Jim Gallery

It takes calm, thoughtful, prayerful meditation on the Word to extract its deepest nourishment.

Vance Havner

The Scriptures were not given for our information, but for our transformation.

D. L. Moody

To everything there is a season, a time for every purpose under heaven.

Ecclesiastes 3:1 NKJV

Trust God's Timing

Sometimes, the hardest thing to do is to wait. This is especially true when we're in a hurry and when we want things to happen now, if not sooner! But God's plan does not always happen in the way that we would like or at the time of our own choosing. Our task—as thoughtful men and women who trust in a benevolent, all-knowing Father—is to wait patiently for God to reveal Himself.

We humans know precisely what we want, and we know exactly when we want it. But, God has a far better plan for each of us. He has created a world that unfolds according to His own timetable, not ours . . . thank goodness! And if we're wise, we trust Him and we wait patiently for Him. After all, He is trustworthy, and He always knows best.

More Great Ideas About God's Timing

When our plans are interrupted, his are not. His plans are proceeding exactly as scheduled, moving us always—including those minutes or hours or years which seem most useless or wasted or unendurable—toward the goal of true maturity.

Elisabeth Elliot

The stops of a good man are ordered by the Lord as well as his steps.

George Mueller

Grass that is here today and gone tomorrow does not require much time to mature. A big oak tree that lasts for generations requires much more time to grow and mature. God is concerned about your life through eternity. Allow Him to take all the time He needs to shape you for His purposes. Larger assignments will require longer periods of preparation.

Henry Blackaby

Have patience. There is no time that is not God's time.

Criswell Freeman

God does not promise to keep us out of the storms and floods, but He does promise to sustain us in the storm, and then bring us out in due time for His glory when the storm has done its work.

Warren Wiersbe

God's delays and His ways can be confusing because the process God uses to accomplish His will can go against human logic and common sense.

Anne Graham Lotz

When we read of the great Biblical leaders, we see that it was not uncommon for God to ask them to wait, not just a day or two, but for years, until God was ready for them to act.

Gloria Gaither

He wants us to have a faith that does not complain while waiting, but rejoices because we know our times are in His hands—nail-scarred hands that labor for our highest good.

Kay Arthur

Finally, brethren, whatever things are true, whatever things are noble, whatever things are just, whatever things are pure, whatever things are lovely, whatever things are of good report, if there is any virtue and if there is anything praiseworthy— meditate on these things.

Philippians 4:8 NKJV

The Direction of Your Thoughts

How will you direct your thoughts today? Will you obey the words of Philippians 4:8 by dwelling upon those things that are true, noble, and just? Or will you allow your thoughts to be hijacked by the negativity that seems to dominate our troubled world?

Are you fearful, angry, bored, or worried? Are you so preoccupied with the concerns of this day that you fail to thank God for the promise of eternity? Are you confused, bitter, or pessimistic? If so, God wants to have a little talk with you.

God intends that you be an ambassador for Him, an enthusiastic, hope-filled Christian. But God won't force you to adopt a positive attitude. It's up to you to think positively about your blessings and opportunities . . . or not. So, today and every day hereafter, celebrate this life that God has given you by focusing your thoughts and your energies upon "things that are excellent and worthy of praise." Today, count your blessings instead of your hardships. And thank the Giver of all things good for gifts that are simply too numerous to count.

It is the thoughts and intents of the heart that shape a person's life.

—

John Eldredge

More Great Ideas About Your Thoughts

Preoccupy my thoughts with your praise beginning today.

Joni Eareckson Tada

Attitude is the mind's paintbrush; it can color any situation.

Barbara Johnson

Whether we think of, or speak to, God, whether we act or suffer for him, all is prayer when we have no other object than his love and the desire of pleasing him.

John Wesley

Beware of cut-and-dried theologies that reduce the ways of God to a manageable formula that keeps life safe. God often does the unexplainable just to keep us on our toes—and also on our knees.

Warren Wiersbe

As we have by faith said no to sin, so we should by faith say yes to God and set our minds on things above, where Christ is seated in the heavenlies.

Vonette Bright

I have come as a light into the world, that whoever believes in Me should not abide in darkness.

John 12:46 NKJV

Jesus Is the Light

The words of John 12:46 teach us that Jesus is the light of the world. And, John 14:6-7 instructs us that Jesus is, "the way, the truth, and the life." Without Christ, we are as far removed from salvation as the east is removed from the west. And without Christ, we can never know the ultimate truth: God's truth.

Truth is God's way: He commands that His believers live in truth, and He rewards those who do so. Jesus is the personification of God's liberating truth, a truth that offers salvation to mankind.

Do you seek to walk with God? Do you seek to feel His presence and His peace? Then you must walk in truth; you must walk in the light; you must walk with the Savior. There is simply no other way.

More Great Ideas About Jesus

I am truly happy with Jesus Christ. I couldn't live without Him. When my life gets beyond the ability to cope, He takes over.

Ruth Bell Graham

There was One, who for "us sinners and our salvation," left the glories of heaven and sojourned upon this earth in weariness and woe, amid those who hated his and finally took his life.

Lottie Moon

The key to my understanding of the Bible is a personal relationship to Jesus Christ.

Oswald Chambers

When you can't see him, trust him. Jesus is closer than you ever dreamed.

Max Lucado

Jesus—personally, socially, politically, the supreme center of human interest today.

R. G. Lee

Jesus Christ is the first and last, author and finisher, beginning and end, alpha and omega, and by Him all other things hold together. He must be first or nothing. God never comes next!

Vance Havner

In your greatest weakness, turn to your greatest strength, Jesus, and hear Him say, "My grace is sufficient for you, for My strength is made perfect in weakness" (2 Corinthians 12:9 NKJV).

Lisa Whelchel

Christians see sin for what it is: willful rebellion against the rulership of God in their lives. And in turning from their sin, they have embraced God's only means of dealing with sin: Jesus.

Kay Arthur

When we are in a situation where Jesus is all we have, we soon discover he is all we really need.

Gigi Graham Tchividjian

Jesus: the proof of God's love.

Philip Yancey

Cast thy burden upon the LORD, and he shall sustain thee: he shall never suffer the righteous to be moved.

Psalm 55:22 KJV

Where to Place Your Burdens

God's Word contains promises upon which we, as Christians, can and must depend. The Bible is a priceless gift, a tool that God intends for us to use in every aspect of our lives. Too many Christians, however, keep their spiritual tool kits tightly closed and out of sight.

Psalm 55:22 instructs us to cast our burdens upon the Lord. And that's perfect advice for men, women, and children alike.

Are you tired? Discouraged? Fearful? Be comforted and trust the promises that God has made to you. Are you worried or anxious? Be confident in God's power. He will never desert you. Do you see a difficult future ahead? Be courageous and call upon God. He will protect you and then use you according to His purposes. Are you confused? Listen to the quiet voice of your Heavenly Father. He is not a God of confusion. Talk with Him; listen to Him; trust Him, and trust His promises.

More Great Ideas About God's Support

God uses our most stumbling, faltering faith-steps as the open door to His doing for us "more than we ask or think."

Catherine Marshall

Measure the size of the obstacles against the size of God.

Beth Moore

He stands fast as your rock, steadfast as your safeguard, sleepless as your watcher, valiant as your champion.

C. H. Spurgeon

Faith is not merely you holding on to God—it is God holding on to you.

E. Stanley Jones

The last and greatest lesson that the soul has to learn is the fact that God, and God alone, is enough for all its needs. This is the lesson that all His dealings with us are meant to teach; and this is the crowning discovery of our whole Christian life. God is enough!

Hannah Whitall Smith

You will show me the path of life; in Your presence is fullness of joy; at Your right hand are pleasures forevermore.

Psalm 16:11 NKJV

He Will Show You the Path

Life is best lived on purpose. And purpose, like everything else in the universe, begins in the heart of God. Whether you realize it or not, God has a direction for your life, a divine calling, a path along which He intends to lead you. When you welcome God into your heart and establish a genuine relationship with Him, He will begin—and He will continue—to make His purposes known.

Each morning, as the sun rises in the east, you welcome a new day, one that is filled to the brim with opportunities, with possibilities, and with God. As you contemplate God's blessings in your own life, you should prayerfully seek His guidance for the day ahead.

Discovering God's unfolding purpose for your life is a daily journey, a journey guided by the teachings of God's Holy Word. As you reflect upon God's promises and upon the meaning that those promises hold for you, ask God to lead you throughout the coming day. Let your Heavenly Father direct your steps; concentrate on what God wants you to do now, and leave the distant future in hands that are far more capable than your own: His hands.

Sometimes, God's intentions will be clear to you; other times, God's plan will seem uncertain at best. But even on those difficult days when you are unsure which way to turn, you must never lose sight of these overriding facts: God created you for a reason; He has important work for you to do; and He's waiting patiently for you to do it. So why not begin today?

Without God, life has no purpose, and without purpose, life has no meaning.

—

Rick Warren

More Great Ideas About
Living on Purpose

His life is our light—our purpose and meaning and reason for living.

Anne Graham Lotz

Yesterday is just experience but tomorrow is glistening with purpose—and today is the channel leading from one to the other.

Barbara Johnson

When God speaks to you through the Bible, prayer, circumstances, the church, or in some other way, he has a purpose in mind for your life.

Henry Blackaby and Claude King

Continually restate to yourself what the purpose of your life is.

Oswald Chambers

Whatever purpose motivates your life, it must be something big enough and grand enough to make the investment worthwhile.

Warren Wiersbe

Now by this we know that we know Him, if we keep His commandments.

1 John 2:3 NKJV

Obedience Now

Obedience to God is determined, not by words, but by deeds. Talking about righteousness is easy; living righteously is far more difficult, especially in today's temptation-filled world.

Since God created Adam and Eve, we human beings have been rebelling against our Creator. Why? Because we are unwilling to trust God's Word, and we are unwilling to follow His commandments. God has given us a guidebook for righteous living called the Holy Bible. It contains thorough instructions which, if followed, lead to fulfillment, abundance, and salvation. But, if we choose to ignore God's commandments, the results are as predictable as they are tragic.

When we seek righteousness in our own lives—and when we seek the companionship of those who do likewise—we reap the spiritual rewards that God intends for our lives. When we behave ourselves as godly men and women, we honor God. When we live righteously and according to God's commandments, He blesses us in ways that we cannot fully understand.

Do you seek God's peace and His blessings? Then obey Him. When you're faced with a difficult choice or a powerful temptation, seek God's counsel and trust the counsel He gives. Invite God into your heart and live according to His commandments. When you do, you will be blessed today, and tomorrow, and forever.

God uses ordinary people who are obedient to Him to do extraordinary things.

—

John Maxwell

More Great Ideas About Obedience

The cross that Jesus commands you and me to carry is the cross of submissive obedience to the will of God, even when His will includes suffering and hardship and things we don't want to do.

Anne Graham Lotz

You may not always see immediate results, but all God wants is your obedience and faithfulness.

Vonette Bright

Obedience is the outward expression of your love of God.

Henry Blackaby

Believe and do what God says. The life-changing consequences will be limitless, and the results will be confidence and peace of mind.

Franklin Graham

We cannot rely on God's promises without obeying his commandments.

John Calvin

So teach us to number our days, that we may gain a heart of wisdom.

Psalm 90:12 NKJV

The Gift of Life

Life is a glorious gift from God. Treat it that way.

This day, like every other, is filled to the brim with opportunities, challenges, and choices. But, no choice that you make is more important than the choice you make concerning God. Today, you will either place Him at the center of your life—or not—and the consequences of that choice have implications that are both temporal and eternal.

Sometimes, we don't intentionally neglect God; we simply allow ourselves to become overwhelmed with the demands of everyday life. And then, without our even realizing it, we gradually drift away from the One we need most. Thankfully, God never drifts away from us. He remains always present, always steadfast, always loving.

As you begin this day, place God and His Son where they belong: in your head, in your prayers, on your lips, and in your heart. And then, with God as your guide and companion, let the journey begin . . .

More Great Ideas About Life

You have a glorious future in Christ! Live every moment in His power and love.

Vonette Bright

As I contemplate all the sacrifices required in order to live a life that is totally focused on Jesus Christ and His eternal kingdom, the joy seeps out of my heart onto my face in a smile of deep satisfaction.

Anne Graham Lotz

The value of a life can only be estimated by its relationship to God.

Oswald Chambers

Jesus wants Life for us, Life with a capital L.

John Eldredge

Our Lord is the Bread of Life. His proportions are perfect. There never was too much or too little of anything about Him. Feed on Him for a well-balanced ration. All the vitamins and calories are there.

Vance Havner

Your life is not a boring stretch of highway. It's a straight line to heaven. And just look at the fields ripening along the way. Look at the tenacity and endurance. Look at the grains of righteousness. You'll have quite a crop at harvest…so don't give up!

Joni Eareckson Tada

The world has never been stable. Jesus Himself was born into the cruelest and most unstable of worlds. No, we have babies and keep trusting and living because the Resurrection is true! The Resurrection was not just a one-time event in history; it is a principle built into the very fabric of our beings, a fact reverberating from every cell of creation: Life wins! Life wins!

Gloria Gaither

A life lived without reflection can be very superficial and empty.

Elisabeth Elliot

The whole point of this life is the healing of the heart's eye through which God is seen.

St. Augustine

Now godliness with contentment is great gain. For we brought nothing into this world, and it is certain we can carry nothing out. And having food and clothing, with these we shall be content.

1 Timothy 6:6-8 NKJV

Keep It Simple

You live in a world where simplicity is in short supply. Think for a moment about the complexity of your everyday life and compare it to the lives of your ancestors. Certainly, you are the beneficiary of many technological innovations, but those innovations have a price: in all likelihood, your world is highly complex. Consider the following:

1. From the moment you wake up in the morning until the time you lay your head on the pillow at night, you are the target of an endless stream of advertising information. Each message is intended to grab your attention in order to convince you to purchase things you didn't know you needed (and probably don't!).

2. Essential aspects of your life, including personal matters such as health care, are subject to an ever-increasing flood of rules and regulations.

3. Unless you take firm control of your time and your life, you may be overwhelmed by an ever-increasing tidal wave of complexity that threatens your happiness.

Your Heavenly Father understands the joy of living simply, and so should you. So do yourself a favor: keep your life as simple as possible. Simplicity is, indeed, genius. By simplifying your life, you are destined to improve it.

More Great Ideas About Simplicity

There is absolutely no evidence that complexity and materialism lead to happiness. On the contrary, there is plenty of evidence that simplicity and spirituality lead to joy, a blessedness that is better than happiness.

Dennis Swanberg

Efficiency is enhanced not by what we accomplish but more often by what we relinquish.

Charles Swindoll

A peaceful heart finds joy in all of life's simple pleasures.

Anonymous

We Christians must simplify our lives or lose untold treasures on earth and in eternity. Modern civilization is so complex as to make the devotional life all but impossible. The need for solitude and quietness was never greater than it is today.

A. W. Tozer

Prescription for a happier and healthier life: resolve to slow down your pace; learn to say no gracefully; resist the temptation to chase after more pleasure, more hobbies, and more social entanglements.

James Dobson

The most powerful life is the most simple life. The most powerful life is the life that knows where it's going, that knows where the source of strength is; it is the life that stays free of clutter and happenstance and hurriedness.

Max Lucado

In the name of Jesus Christ who was never in a hurry, we pray, O God, that You will slow us down, for we know that we live too fast. With all eternity before us, make us take time to live—time to get acquainted with You, time to enjoy Your blessing, and time to know each other.

Peter Marshall

Therefore, whether you eat or drink, or whatever you do, do all to the glory of God.

1 Corinthians 10:31 NKJV

His Priorities and Your Health

When it comes to matters of physical, spiritual, and emotional health, Christians possess an infallible guidebook: the Holy Bible. And, when it comes to matters concerning fitness—whether physical, emotional, or spiritual fitness—God's Word can help us establish clear priorities that can guide our steps and our lives.

It's easy to talk about establishing clear priorities for maintaining physical and spiritual health, but it's much more difficult to live according to those priorities. For busy believers living in a demanding world, placing first things first can be difficult indeed. Why? Because so many people are expecting so many things from us!

If you're having trouble prioritizing your day—or if you're having trouble sticking to a plan that enhances your spiritual and physical health—perhaps you've been trying to organize your life according to your own plans, not God's. A better strategy, of course, is to take your daily obligations and place them in the hands of the One who created you. To do so, you must prioritize your day according to God's commandments, and you must seek His will and His wisdom in all matters.

Would you like to embark upon a personal journey to better fitness? If so, you should remind yourself that on every step of that journey, you have a traveling companion: your Heavenly Father. Turn the concerns of this day over to Him—prayerfully, earnestly, and often. And trust Him to give you the strength you need to become the kind of person He wants you to become.

God wants you to give Him your body. Some people do foolish things with their bodies. God wants your body as a holy sacrifice.

—

Warren Wiersbe

More Great Ideas About Health

If you want to form a new habit, get to work. If you want to break a bad habit, get on your knees.

Marie T. Freeman

People are funny. When they are young, they will spend their health to get wealth. Later, they will gladly pay all they have trying to get their health back.

John Maxwell

Our primary motivation should not be for more energy or to avoid a heart attack but to please God with our bodies.

Carole Lewis

The key to healthy eating is moderation and managing what you eat every day.

John Maxwell

Ultimate healing and the glorification of the body are certainly among the blessings of Calvary for the believing Christian. Immediate healing is not guaranteed.

Warren Wiersbe

Man does not see what the Lord sees, for man sees what is visible, but the Lord sees the heart.

1 Samuel 16:7 HCSB

Keeping Up Appearances

The words of 1 Samuel 16:7 remind us God sees the heart. We human beings, on the other hand, are often far more concerned with outward appearances.

Are you worried about keeping up appearances? And as a result, do you spend too much time, energy, or money on things that are intended to make you look good? If so, you are certainly not alone. Ours is a society that focuses intently upon appearances. We are told time and again that we can't be "too thin or too rich." But in truth, the important things in life have little to do with food, fashion, fame, or fortune.

Today, spend less time trying to please the world and more time trying to please your earthly family and your Father in heaven. Focus on pleasing God and your loved ones, and don't worry too much about trying to impress the folks you happen to pass on the street. It takes too much energy—and too much life—to keep up appearances. So don't waste your energy or your life.

More Great Ideas About Appearances

Our ultimate aim in life is not to be healthy, wealthy, prosperous, or problem free. Our ultimate aim in life is to bring glory to God.

Anne Graham Lotz

Once you loosen up, let yourself be who you are: the wonderful, witty woman whom God will use to encourage and uplift other people.

Barbara Johnson

Being loved by Him whose opinion matters most gives us the security to risk loving, too—even loving ourselves.

Gloria Gaither

Outside appearances, things like the clothes you wear or the car you drive, are important to other people but totally unimportant to God. Trust God.

Marie T. Freeman

Comparison is the root of all feelings of inferiority.

James Dobson

Fashion is an enduring testimony to the fact that we live quite consciously before the eyes of others.

John Eldredge

Those who follow the crowd usually get lost in it.

Rick Warren

The single most important element in any human relationship is honesty—with oneself, with God, and with others.

Catherine Marshall

If the narrative of the Scriptures teaches us anything, from the serpent in the Garden to the carpenter in Nazareth, it teaches us that things are rarely what they seem, that we shouldn't be fooled by appearances.

John Eldredge

It is impossible to please everybody. It's not impossible to please God. So try pleasing God.

Jim Gallery

Whoever conceals an offense promotes love, but whoever gossips about it separates friends.

Proverbs 17:9 HCSB

Above and Beyond Gossip

The Bible clearly tells us that gossip is wrong. But when it comes to the special confidences that you share with your very closest friends, gossip can be disastrous.

The Bible reminds us that "Reckless words pierce like a sword, but the tongue of the wise brings healing" (Proverbs 12:18 NIV). Therefore, if we are to solve more problems than we start, we must measure our words carefully, and we must never betray a confidence. But sometimes even the most thoughtful among us may speak first and think second (with decidedly mixed results).

When we speak too quickly, we may say things that that would be better left unsaid. When we forgo the wonderful opportunity to consider our thoughts before we give voice to them, we're putting ourselves and our relationships in danger.

A far better strategy, of course, is to do the more difficult thing: to think first and to speak next. When we do so, we give ourselves ample time to compose our thoughts and to consult our Creator before we say something that we might soon regret.

More Great Ideas About Gossip

It is time that the followers of Jesus revise their language and learn to speak respectfully of non-Christian peoples.

Lottie Moon

When you talk, choose the very same words that you would use if Jesus were looking over your shoulder. Because He is.

Marie T. Freeman

Like dynamite, God's power is only latent power until it is released. You can release God's dynamite power into people's lives and the world through faith, your words, and prayer.

Bill Bright

The great test of a man's character is his tongue.

Oswald Chambers

Fill the heart with the love of Christ so that only truth and purity can come out of the mouth.

Warren Wiersbe

A little kindly advice is better than a great deal of scolding.

Fanny Crosby

The things that we feel most deeply we ought to learn to be silent about, at least until we have talked them over thoroughly with God.

Elisabeth Elliot

If you can't think of something nice to say, keep thinking.

Criswell Freeman

I still believe we ought to talk about Jesus. The old country doctor of my boyhood days always began his examination by saying, "Let me see your tongue." That's a good way to check a Christian: the tongue test. Let's hear what he is talking about.

Vance Havner

Change the heart, and you change the speech.

Warren Wiersbe

The sensible see danger and take cover; the foolish keep going and are punished.

Proverbs 27:12 HCSB

Plan Ahead . . . and Work Hard

Are you willing to plan for the future—and are you willing to work diligently to accomplish the plans that you've made? The Book of Proverbs teaches that the plans of hardworking people (like you) are rewarded.

If you desire to reap a bountiful harvest from life, you must plan for the future while entrusting the final outcome to God. Then, you must do your part to make the future better (by working dutifully), while acknowledging the sovereignty of God's hands over all affairs, including your own.

Are you in a hurry for success to arrive at your doorstep? Don't be. Instead, work carefully, plan thoughtfully, and wait patiently. Remember that you're not the only one working on your behalf: God, too, is at work. And with Him as your partner, your ultimate success is guaranteed.

More Great Ideas About Planning

The only way you can experience abundant life is to surrender your plans to Him.

Charles Stanley

Allow your dreams a place in your prayers and plans. God-given dreams can help you move into the future He is preparing for you.

Barbara Johnson

God has a plan for your life . . . do you?

Criswell Freeman

You can't start building a better tomorrow if you wait till tomorrow to start building.

Marie T. Freeman

When you become consumed by God's call on your life, everything will take on new meaning and significance. You will begin to see every facet of your life—including your pain—as a means through which God can work to bring others to Himself.

Charles Swindoll

We are not necessarily doubting that God will do the best for us; we are wondering how painful the best will turn out to be.

C. S. Lewis

Plan ahead—it wasn't raining when Noah built the ark.

Anonymous

Our problem is that we become too easily enamored with our own plans.

Henry Blackaby

We should not be upset when unexpected and upsetting things happen. God, in his wisdom, means to make something of us which we have not yet attained, and He is dealing with us accordingly.

J. I. Packer

Our heavenly Father never takes anything from his children unless he means to give them something better.

George Mueller

*I have set before you life and death, blessing and curse.
Choose life so that you and your descendants may live, love
the Lord your God, obey Him, and remain faithful to Him.
For He is your life, and He will prolong your life in the land
the Lord swore to give to your fathers Abraham, Isaac, and
Jacob.*

Deuteronomy 30:19-20 HCSB

Making Good Choices

L ife is a series of choices. From the instant we wake
in the morning until the moment we nod off to
sleep at night, we make countless decisions: decisions about the things we do, decisions about the words
we speak, and decisions about the thoughts we choose to
think. Simply put, the quality of those decisions determines the quality of our lives.

As believers who have been saved by a loving and
merciful God, we have every reason to make wise choices. Yet sometimes, amid the inevitable hustle and bustle
of life here on earth, we allow ourselves to behave in
ways that we know are displeasing to God. When we do,
we forfeit—albeit temporarily—the joy and the peace
that we might otherwise experience through Him.

As you consider the next step in your life's journey,
take time to consider how many things in this life you

can control: your thoughts, your words, your priorities, and your actions, for starters. And then, if you sincerely want to discover God's purpose for your life, make choices that are pleasing to Him. He deserves no less . . . and neither do you.

Every time you make a choice, you are turning the central part of you, the part that chooses, into something a little different from what it was before.

—

C. S. Lewis

More Great Ideas About Choices

Every day of our lives we make choices about how we're going to live that day.

Luci Swindoll

There may be no trumpet sound or loud applause when we make a right decision, just a calm sense of resolution and peace.

Gloria Gaither

Commitment to His lordship on Easter, at revivals, or even every Sunday is not enough. We must choose this day—and every day—whom we will serve. This deliberate act of the will is the inevitable choice between habitual fellowship and habitual failure.

Beth Moore

Life is pretty much like a cafeteria line—it offers us many choices, both good and bad. The Christian must have a spiritual radar that detects the difference not only between bad and good but also among good, better, and best.

Dennis Swanberg

Be sober! Be on the alert! Your adversary the Devil is prowling around like a roaring lion, looking for anyone he can devour.

1 Peter 5:8 HCSB

Be Alert for the Adversary

Sometimes sin has a way of sneaking up on us. In the beginning, we don't intend to rebel against God—in fact, we don't think much about God at all. We think, instead, about the allure of sin, and we think (quite incorrectly) that sin is "harmless."

If we deny our sins, we allow those sins to flourish. And if we allow sinful behaviors to become habits, we invite certain hardships into our own lives and into the lives of our loved ones.

Sin tears down character. When we yield to the distractions and temptations of this troubled world, we suffer. But God has other intentions, and His plans for our lives do not include sin or denial.

As creatures of free will, we may disobey God whenever we choose, but when we do so, we put ourselves and our loved ones in peril. Why? Because disobedience invites disaster. We cannot sin against God without consequence. We cannot live outside His will without injury.

We cannot distance ourselves from God without hardening our hearts. We cannot yield to the ever-tempting distractions of our world and, at the same time, enjoy God's peace.

Sometimes, in a futile attempt to justify our behaviors, we make a distinction between "big" sins and "little" ones. To do so is a mistake of "big" proportions. Sins of all shapes and sizes have the power to do us great harm. And in a world where sin is big business, that's certainly a sobering thought.

We cannot out-sin God's ability to forgive us.

—

Beth Moore

More Great Ideas About Sin

Repentance is a complete surrender of my sinfulness to the only One who can cleanse me from all sin, and that is Jesus Christ.

Elisabeth Elliot

Could it be that the greatest sin is simply not to love the Lord your God with all your heart, mind, soul, and strength?

Anne Graham Lotz

Our Savior kneels down and gazes upon the darkest acts of our lives. But rather than recoil in horror, he reaches out in kindness and says, "I can clean that if you want." And from the basin of his grace, he scoops a palm full of mercy and washes our sin.

Max Lucado

There is nothing wrong with asking God's direction. But it is wrong to go our own way, then expect Him to bail us out.

Larry Burkett

Therefore, if anyone is in Christ, he is a new creation; old things have passed away; behold, all things have become new.

2 Corinthians 5:17 NKJV

The New You

In 2 Corinthians 5:17, we are told that when a person accepts Christ, he or she becomes a new creation. Have you invited God's Son to reign over your heart and your life? If so, think for a moment about the "old" you, the person you were before you invited Christ into your heart. Now, think about the "new" you, the person you have become since then. Is there a difference between the "old" you and the "new and improved" version? There should be! And that difference should be noticeable not only to you but also to others.

Warren Wiersbe observed, "The greatest miracle of all is the transformation of a lost sinner into a child of God." And Oswald Chambers noted, "If the Spirit of God has transformed you within, you will exhibit Divine characteristics in your life, not good human characteristics. God's life in us expresses itself as God's life, not as a human life trying to be godly."

When you invited Christ to reign over your heart, you became a new creation through Him. This day offers yet another opportunity to behave yourself like that new creation by serving your Creator and strengthening your character. When you do, God will guide your steps and bless your endeavors today and forever.

More Great Ideas About Conversion

The amazing thing about Jesus is that He doesn't just patch up our lives, He gives us a brand new sheet, a clean slate to start over, all new.

Gloria Gaither

Be filled with the Holy Spirit; join a church where the members believe the Bible and know the Lord; seek the fellowship of other Christians; learn and be nourished by God's Word and His many promises. Conversion is not the end of your journey—it is only the beginning.

Corrie ten Boom

Has he taken over your heart? Perhaps he resides there, but does he preside there?

Vance Havner

No one can be converted except with the consent of his own free will because God does not override human choice.

Billy Graham

We had better quickly discover whether we have mere religion or a real experience with Jesus, whether we have outward observance of religious forms or hearts that beat in tune with God.

Jim Cymbala

If we accept His invitation to salvation, we live with Him forever. However, if we do not accept because we refuse His only Son as our Savior, then we exclude ourselves from My Father's House. It's our choice.

Anne Graham Lotz

If you are God's child, you are no longer bound to your past or to what you were. You are a brand new creature in Christ Jesus.

Kay Arthur

Being born again is God's solution to our need for love and life and light.

Anne Graham Lotz

But Jesus looked at them and said to them, "With men this is impossible, but with God all things are possible."

Matthew 19:26 NKJV

All Things Are Possible

Sometimes, because we are imperfect human beings with limited understanding and limited faith, we place limitations on God. But, God's power has no limitations. God will work miracles in our lives if we trust Him with everything we have and everything we are. When we do, we experience the miraculous results of His endless love and His awesome power.

Miracles, both great and small, are an integral part of everyday life, but usually, we are too busy or too cynical to notice God's handiwork. We don't expect to see miracles, so we simply overlook them.

Do you lack the faith that God can work miracles in your own life? If so, it's time to reconsider. If you have allowed yourself to become a "doubting Thomas," you are attempting to place limitations on a God who has none. Instead of doubting your Heavenly Father, you must trust Him. Then, you must wait and watch . . . because something miraculous is going to happen to you, and it might just happen today.

More Great Ideas About Miracles

When we face an impossible situation, all self-reliance and self-confidence must melt away; we must be totally dependent on Him for the resources.

Anne Graham Lotz

There is Someone who makes possible what seems completely impossible.

Catherine Marshall

Only God can move mountains, but faith and prayer can move God.

E. M. Bounds

I have been suspected of being what is called a fundamentalist. That is because I never regard any narrative as unhistorical simply on the ground that it includes the miraculous.

C. S. Lewis

We have a God who delights in impossibilities.

Andrew Murray

Never be afraid to hope—or to ask—for a miracle.

Criswell Freeman

I could go through this day oblivious to the miracles all around me or I could tune in and "enjoy."

Gloria Gaither

Here lies the tremendous mystery—that God should be all-powerful, yet refuse to coerce. He summons us to cooperation. We are honored in being given the opportunity to participate in His good deeds. Remember how He asked for help in performing His miracles: Fill the water pots, stretch out your hand, distribute the loaves.

Elisabeth Elliot

Are you looking for a miracle? If you keep your eyes wide open and trust in God, you won't have to look very far.

Marie T. Freeman

The miracles in fact are a retelling in small letters of the very same story which is written across the whole world in letters too large for some of us to see.

C. S. Lewis

He did it with all his heart. So he prospered.

2 Chronicles 31:21 NKJV

Putting Yourself and Your Heart into Your Work

The old adage is both familiar and true: We must pray as if everything depended upon God, but work as if everything depended upon us. Yet sometimes, when we are weary and discouraged, we may allow our worries to sap our energy and our hope. God has other intentions. God intends that we pray for things, and He intends that we be willing to work for the things that we pray for. More importantly, God intends that our work should become His work.

Whether you're in school or in the workplace, your success will depend, in large part, upon the passion that you bring to your work. God has created a world in which diligence is rewarded and sloth is not. So whatever you choose to do, do it with commitment, with excitement, with enthusiasm, and with vigor.

God did not create you for a life of mediocrity; He created you for far greater things. Reaching for greater things usually requires work and lots of it, which is perfectly fine with God. After all, He knows that you're up to the task, and He has big plans for you. Very big plans.

Success or failure can be
pretty well predicted by
the degree to which
the heart is fully in it.

—

John Eldredge

More Great Ideas About Passion

Life is too short to spend it being angry, bored, or dull.

Barbara Johnson

One of the great needs in the church today is for every Christian to become enthusiastic about his faith in Jesus Christ.

Billy Graham

If your heart has grown cold, it is because you have moved away from the fire of His presence.

Beth Moore

Everything you love is what makes a life worth living.

John Eldredge

We honor God by asking for great things when they are part of His promise. We dishonor Him and cheat ourselves when we ask for molehills where He has offered mountains.

Vance Havner

In fact, when we were with you, this is what we commanded
you: "If anyone isn't willing to work, he should not eat."

2 Thessalonians 3:10 HCSB

We're Expected to Work

God's Word teaches us the value of hard work. In his second letter to the 2 Thessalonians, Paul warns, "If anyone isn't willing to work, he should not eat." And the Book of Proverbs proclaims, "One who is slack in his work is brother to one who destroys" (18:9 NIV). In short, God has created a world in which diligence is rewarded but sloth is not. So, whatever it is that you choose to do, do it with commitment, excitement, and vigor.

Hard work is not simply a proven way to get ahead; it's also part of God's plan for you. God did not create you for a life of mediocrity; He created you for far greater things. Reaching for greater things usually requires work and lots of it, which is perfectly fine with God. After all, He knows that you're up to the task, and He has big plans for you if you possess a loving heart and willing hands.

More Great Ideas About Work

You can't climb the ladder of life with your hands in your pockets.

Barbara Johnson

Great relief and satisfaction can come from seeking God's priorities for us in each season, discerning what is "best" in the midst of many noble opportunities, and pouring our most excellent energies into those things.

Beth Moore

If you honor God with your work, He will honor you because of your work.

Marie T. Freeman

Ordinary work, which is what most of us do most of the time, is ordained by God every bit as much as is the extraordinary.

Elisabeth Elliot

The world does not consider labor a blessing, therefore it flees and hates it, but the pious who fear the Lord labor with a ready and cheerful heart, for they know God's command, and they acknowledge His calling.

Martin Luther

Few things fire up a person's commitment like dedication to excellence.

John Maxwell

In the very place where God has put us, whatever its limitations, whatever kind of work it may be, we may indeed serve the Lord Christ.

Elisabeth Elliot

We must trust as if it all depended on God and work as if it all depended on us.

C. H. Spurgeon

Thank God every morning when you get up that you have something which must be done, whether you like it or not. Work breeds a hundred virtues that idleness never knows.

Charles Kingsley

It may be that the day of judgment will dawn tomorrow; in that case, we shall gladly stop working for a better tomorrow. But not before.

Dietrich Bonhoeffer

Unless the Lord builds a house, its builders labor over it in vain; unless the Lord watches over a city, the watchman stays alert in vain.

Psalm 127:1 HCSB

He Watches Over Us

Have you ever faced challenges that seemed too big to handle? Have you ever faced big problems that, despite your best efforts, simply could not be solved? If so, you know how uncomfortable it is to feel helpless in the face of difficult circumstances. Thankfully, even when there's nowhere else to turn, you can turn your thoughts and prayers to God, and He will respond.

God's hand uplifts those who turn their hearts and prayers to Him. Count yourself among that number. When you do, you can live courageously and joyfully, knowing that "this too will pass"—but that God's love for you will not. And you can draw strength from the knowledge that you are a marvelous creation, loved, protected, and uplifted by the ever-present hand of God.

More Great Ideas About God's Protection

In all the old castles of England, there was a place called the keep. It was always the strongest and best protected place in the castle, and in it were hidden all who were weak and helpless and unable to defend themselves in times of danger. Shall we be afraid to hide ourselves in the keeping power of our Divine Keeper, who neither slumbers nor sleeps, and who has promised to preserve our going out and our coming in, from this time forth and even forever more?

Hannah Whitall Smith

There is no safer place to live than the center of His will.

Calvin Miller

When you fall and skin your knees and skin your heart, He'll pick you up.

Charles Stanley

My case is urgent, and I do not see how I am to be delivered; but this is no business of mine. He who makes the promise will find ways and means of keeping it. It is mine to obey His command; it is not mine to direct His counsels. I am His servant, not His solicitor. I call upon Him, and He will deliver.

C. H. Spurgeon

God delights in spreading His protective wings and enfolding His frightened, weary, beaten-down, worn-out children.

Bill Hybels

Trials are not enemies of faith but opportunities to reveal God's faithfulness.

Barbara Johnson

Gather the riches of God's promises which can strengthen you in the time when there will be no freedom.

Corrie ten Boom

Our future may look fearfully intimidating, yet we can look up to the Engineer of the Universe, confident that nothing escapes His attention or slips out of the control of those strong hands.

Elisabeth Elliot

Through all of the crises of life—and we all are going to experience them—we have this magnificent Anchor.

Franklin Graham

Give thanks to the Lord, for He is good; His faithful love endures forever.

Psalm 106:1 HCSB

His Love Endures

God's love for you is bigger and better than you can imagine. In fact, God's love is far too big to comprehend (in this lifetime). But this much we know: God loves you so much that He sent His Son Jesus to come to this earth and to die for you. And, when you accepted Jesus into your heart, God gave you a gift that is more precious than gold: the gift of eternal life. Now, precisely because you are a wondrous creation treasured by God, a question presents itself: What will you do in response to God's love? Will you ignore it or embrace it? Will you return it or neglect it? The decision, of course, is yours and yours alone.

When you embrace God's love, you are forever changed. When you embrace God's love, you feel differently about yourself, your neighbors, and your world. When you embrace God's love, you share His message and you obey His commandments.

When you accept the Father's gift of grace, you are blessed here on earth and throughout all eternity. So do yourself a favor right now: accept God's love with open arms and welcome His Son Jesus into your heart. When you do, your life will be changed today, tomorrow, and forever.

More Great Ideas About God's Love

Being loved by Him whose opinion matters most gives us the security to risk loving, too—even loving ourselves.

Gloria Gaither

There is no pit so deep that God's love is not deeper still.

Corrie ten Boom

I think God knew that the message we sometimes need to hear today is not what a great and mighty God we serve, but rather what a tender, loving Father we have, even when He says no.

Lisa Whelchel

Even when we cannot see the why and wherefore of God's dealings, we know that there is love in and behind them, so we can rejoice always.

J. I. Packer

The fact is, God no longer deals with us in judgment but in mercy. If people got what they deserved, this old planet would have ripped apart at the seams centuries ago. Praise God that because of His great love "we are not consumed, for his compassions never fail" (Lam. 3:22).

Joni Eareckson Tada

God proved his love on the cross. When Christ hung, and bled, and died, it was God saying to the world—I love you.

Billy Graham

The hope we have in Jesus is the anchor for the soul— something sure and steadfast, preventing drifting or giving way, lowered to the depth of God's love.

Franklin Graham

Every tiny bit of my life that has value I owe to the redemption of Jesus Christ. Am I doing anything to enable Him to bring His redemption into evident reality in the lives of others?

Oswald Chambers

No temptation has overtaken you except such as is common to man; but God is faithful, who will not allow you to be tempted beyond what you are able, but with the temptation will also make the way of escape, that you may be able to bear it.

1 Corinthians 10:13 NKJV

Resisting Temptation

It's inevitable: today you will be tempted by somebody or something—in fact, you will probably be tempted many times. Why? Because you live in a world that is filled to the brim with temptations! Some of these temptations are small; eating a second scoop of ice cream, for example, is enticing but not very dangerous. Other temptations, however, are not nearly so harmless.

The devil is working 24/7, and he's causing pain and heartache in more ways than ever before. We, as believers, must remain watchful and strong. And the good news is this: When it comes to fighting Satan, we are never alone. God is always with us, and He gives us the power to resist temptation whenever we ask Him to give us strength.

In a letter to believers, Peter offered a stern warning: "Your adversary, the devil, prowls around like a roaring lion, seeking someone to devour" (1 Peter 5:8 NASB). As Christians, we must take that warning seriously, and we must behave accordingly.

More Great Ideas About Temptation

Instant intimacy is one of the leading warning signals of a seduction.

Beth Moore

Lord, what joy to know that Your powers are so much greater than those of the enemy.

Corrie ten Boom

Flee temptation without leaving a forwarding address.

Barbara Johnson

There is sharp necessity for giving Christ absolute obedience. The devil bids for our complete self-will. To whatever extent we give this self-will the right to be master over our lives, we are, to an extent, giving Satan a toehold.

Catherine Marshall

Since you are tempted without ceasing, pray without ceasing.

C. H. Spurgeon

A man who gives in to temptation after five minutes simply does not know what it would have been like an hour later.

C. S. Lewis

Deception is the enemy's ongoing plan of attack.

Stormie Omartian

It is easier to stay out of temptation than to get out of it.

Rick Warren

In the worst temptations nothing can help us but faith that God's Son has put on flesh, sits at the right hand of the Father, and prays for us. There is no mightier comfort.

Martin Luther

Most Christians do not know or fully realize that the adversary of our lives is Satan and that his main tool is our flesh, our old nature.

Bill Bright

But this I say: He who sows sparingly will also reap sparingly, and he who sows bountifully will also reap bountifully. So let each one give as he purposes in his heart, not grudgingly or of necessity; for God loves a cheerful giver.

2 Corinthians 9:6-7 NKJV

Generosity Now

The thread of generosity is woven—completely and inextricably—into the very fabric of Christ's teachings. As He sent His disciples out to heal the sick and spread God's message of salvation, Jesus offered this guiding principle: "Freely you have received, freely give" (Matthew 10:8 NIV). The principle still applies. If we are to be disciples of Christ, we must give freely of our time, our possessions, and our love.

In 2 Corinthians 9, Paul reminds us that when we sow the seeds of generosity, we reap bountiful rewards in accordance with God's plan for our lives. Thus, we are instructed to give cheerfully and without reservation. So today, make this pledge and keep it: Be a cheerful, generous, courageous giver. The world needs your help, and you need the spiritual rewards that will be yours when you give it.

More Great Ideas About Generosity

Here lies the tremendous mystery—that God should be all-powerful, yet refuse to coerce. He summons us to cooperation. We are honored in being given the opportunity to participate in His good deeds. Remember how He asked for help in performing His miracles: Fill the water pots, stretch out your hand, distribute the loaves.

Elisabeth Elliot

What is your focus today? Joy comes when it is Jesus first, others second . . . then you.

Kay Arthur

God does not supply money to satisfy our every whim and desire. His promise is to meet our needs and provide an abundance so that we can help other people.

Larry Burkett

The measure of a life, after all, is not its duration but its donation.

Corrie ten Boom

Abundant living means abundant giving.

E. Stanley Jones

God does not supply money to satisfy our every whim and desire. His promise is to meet our needs and provide an abundance so that we can help other people.

Larry Burkett

When somebody needs a helping hand, he doesn't need it tomorrow or the next day. He needs it now, and that's exactly when you should offer to help. Good deeds, if they are really good, happen sooner rather than later.

Marie T. Freeman

We are never more like God than when we give.

Charles Swindoll

God does not need our money. But, you and I need the experience of giving it.

James Dobson

The happiest and most joyful people are those who give money and serve.

Dave Ramsey

Should we accept only good from God and not adversity?

Job 2:10 HCSB

Learning the Art of Acceptance

If you're like most people, you like being in control. Period. You want things to happen according to your wishes and according to your timetable. But sometimes, God has other plans . . . and He always has the final word. Job understood the importance of accepting God's sovereignty in good times and bad . . . and so should you.

The American theologian Reinhold Niebuhr composed a profoundly simple verse that came to be known as the Serenity Prayer: "God, grant me the serenity to accept the things I cannot change, the courage to change the things I can, and the wisdom to know the difference." Niebuhr's words are far easier to recite than they are to live by.

Oswald Chambers correctly observed, "Our Lord never asks us to decide for Him; He asks us to yield to Him—a very different matter." These words remind us that even when we cannot understand the workings of God, we must trust Him and accept His will.

Are you embittered by a personal tragedy that you did not deserve and cannot understand? If so, it's time to make peace with life. It's time to forgive others, and, if necessary, to forgive yourself. It's time to accept the unchangeable past, to embrace the priceless present, and to have faith in the promise of tomorrow. It's time to trust God completely. And it's time to reclaim the peace—His peace—that can and should be yours.

So if you've encountered unfortunate circumstances that are beyond your power to control, accept those circumstances . . . and trust God. When you do, you can be comforted in the knowledge that your Creator is both loving and wise, and that He understands His plans perfectly, even when you do not.

I am truly grateful that faith enables me to move past the question of "Why?"

—

Zig Ziglar

More Great Ideas About Acceptance

When we face an impossible situation, all self-reliance and self-confidence must melt away; we must be totally dependent on Him for the resources.

Anne Graham Lotz

I have held many things in my hands, and I have lost them all; but whatever I have placed in God's hands, that I still possess.

Corrie ten Boom

Acceptance says: True, this is my situation at the moment. I'll look unblinkingly at the reality of it. But, I'll also open my hands to accept willingly whatever a loving Father sends me.

Catherine Marshall

Ultimately things work out best for those who make the best of the way things work out.

Barbara Johnson

Trust the past to God's mercy, the present to God's love, and the future to God's providence.

St. Augustine

But be doers of the word, and not hearers only, deceiving yourselves.

James 1:22 NKJV

Actions Speak Louder

The old saying is both familiar and true: actions speak louder than words. And as believers, we must beware: our actions should always give credence to the changes that Christ can make in the lives of those who walk with Him.

God calls upon each of us to act in accordance with His will and with respect for His commandments. If we are to be responsible believers, we must realize that it is never enough simply to hear the instructions of God; we must also live by them. And it is never enough to wait idly by while others do God's work here on earth; we, too, must act. Doing God's work is a responsibility that each of us must bear, and when we do, our loving Heavenly Father rewards our efforts with a bountiful harvest.

Do you seek God's peace and His blessings? Then obey Him. When you're faced with a difficult choice or a powerful temptation, seek God's counsel and trust the counsel He gives. Invite God into your heart and act in accordance with His commandments. When you do, you will be blessed today, and tomorrow, and forever.

More Great Ideas About Taking Action Now

From the very moment one feels called to act is born the strength to bear whatever horror one will feel or see. In some inexplicable way, terror loses its overwhelming power when it becomes a task that must be faced.

Emmi Bonhoeffer

A bird does not know it can fly before it uses its wings. We learn God's love in our hearts as soon as we act upon it.

Corrie ten Boom

We set the sail; God makes the wind.

Anonymous

Never fail to do something because you don't feel like it. Sometimes you just have to do it now, and you'll feel like it later.

Marie T. Freeman

Do noble things, do not dream them all day long.

Charles Kingsley

Paul did one thing. Most of us dabble in forty things. Are you a doer or a dabbler?

Vance Havner

We spend our lives dreaming of the future, not realizing that a little of it slips away every day.

Barbara Johnson

Logic will not change an emotion, but action will.

Zig Ziglar

It's sobering, it's shocking, it's almost beyond belief, but it is 100 percent biblically true: Every one of our actions and attitudes affects God. By His nature He is an expressive God, and he has given us the capability of stirring His heart.

Bill Hybels

The church needs people who are doers of the Word and not just hearers.

Warren Wiersbe

In the same way faith, if it doesn't have works, is dead by itself.

James 2:17 HCSB

Faith Without Works Doesn't Work

The central message of James' letter is the need for believers to act upon their beliefs. James' instruction is clear: "faith without works is dead." We are saved by our faith in Christ, but salvation does not signal the end of our earthly responsibilities; it marks the true beginning of our work for the Lord.

If your faith in God is strong, you will find yourself drawn toward God's work. You will serve Him, not just with words or prayers, but also with deeds. Because of your faith, you will feel compelled to do God's work—to do it gladly, faithfully, joyfully, and consistently.

Today, redouble your efforts to do God's bidding here on earth. Never have the needs—or the opportunities—been greater.

More Great Ideas About Good Works

We are saved by faith alone, but faith is never alone.

John Calvin

Where there are no good works, there is no faith. If works and love do not blossom forth, it is not genuine faith, the Gospel has not yet gained a foothold, and Christ is not yet rightly known.

Martin Luther

The religion of Jesus Christ has an ethical as well as a doctrinal side.

Lottie Moon

It is faith that saves us, not works, but the faith that saves us always produces works.

C. H. Spurgeon

No good work is done anywhere without aid from the Father of Lights.

C. S. Lewis

Blessed are those who hunger and thirst for righteousness, because they will be filled.

Matthew 5:6 HCSB

Living Righteously

Matthew 5:6 teaches us that righteous men and women are blessed. Do you sincerely desire to be a righteous person? Are you bound and determined—despite the inevitable temptations and distractions of our modern age—to be an example of godly behavior to your family, to your friends, to your coworkers, and to your community? If so, you must obey God's commandments. There are no shortcuts and no loopholes—to be a faithful Christian, you must be an obedient Christian.

You will never become righteous by accident. You must hunger for righteousness, and you must ask God to guide your steps. When you ask Him for guidance, He will give it. So, when you're faced with a difficult choice or a powerful temptation, seek God's counsel and trust the counsel He gives. Invite God into your heart and live according to His commandments. When you do, you will be blessed today, tomorrow, and forever.

More Great Ideas About Doing What's Right

Becoming pure is a process of spiritual growth, and taking seriously the confession of sin during prayer time moves that process along, causing us to purge our life of practices that displease God.

Elizabeth George

Holiness has never been the driving force of the majority. It is, however, mandatory for anyone who wants to enter the kingdom.

Elisabeth Elliot

We have a decision to make—to turn away from sin or to be miserable and suffer the consequences of continual disobedience.

Vonette Bright

Our afflictions are designed not to break us but to bend us toward the eternal and the holy.

Barbara Johnson

A man who lives right, and is right, has more power in his silence than another has by his words.

Phillips Brooks

The great thing is to be found at one's post as a child of God, living each day as though it were our last, but planning as though our world might last a hundred years.

C. S. Lewis

He doesn't need an abundance of words. He doesn't need a dissertation about your life. He just wants your attention. He wants your heart.

Kathy Troccoli

Impurity is not just a wrong action; impurity is the state of mind and heart and soul which is just the opposite of purity and wholeness.

A. W. Tozer

Righteousness not only defines God, but God defines righteousness.

Bill Hybels

Have your heart right with Christ, and he will visit you often, and so turn weekdays into Sundays, meals into sacraments, homes into temples, and earth into heaven.

C. H. Spurgeon

Therefore humble yourselves under the mighty hand of God, that He may exalt you in due time, casting all your care upon Him, for He cares for you.

1 Peter 5:6-7 NKJV

He Cares

It is easy to become overwhelmed by the demands of everyday life, but if you're a faithful follower of the One from Galilee, you need never be overwhelmed. Why? Because God's love is sufficient to meet your needs. Whatever dangers you may face, whatever heartbreaks you must endure, God is with you, and He stands ready to comfort you and to heal you.

The Psalmist writes, "Weeping may endure for a night, but joy comes in the morning" (Psalm 30:5 NKJV). But when we are suffering, the morning may seem very far away. It is not. God promises that He is "near to those who have a broken heart" (Psalm 34:18 NKJV).

If you are experiencing the intense pain of a recent loss, or if you are still mourning a loss from long ago, perhaps you are now ready to begin the next stage of your journey with God. If so, be mindful of this fact: the loving heart of God is sufficient to meet any challenge, including yours.

More Great Ideas About God's Support

In God's faithfulness lies eternal security.

Corrie ten Boom

We have ample evidence that the Lord is able to guide. The promises cover every imaginable situation. All we need to do is to take the hand he stretches out.

Elisabeth Elliot

No matter what we are going through, no matter how long the waiting for answers, of one thing we may be sure. God is faithful. He keeps His promises. What He starts, He finishes . . . including His perfect work in us.

Gloria Gaither

God uses our most stumbling, faltering faith-steps as the open door to His doing for us "more than we ask or think."

Catherine Marshall

God's help is near and always available, but it is only given to those who seek it.

Max Lucado

We should learn to live in the presence of the living God. He should be a well for us: delightful, comforting, unfailing, springing up to eternal life (John 4:14). When we rely on other people, their water supplies ultimately dry up. But, the well of the Creator never fails to nourish us.

C. H. Spurgeon

God is bigger than your problems. Whatever worries press upon you today, put them in God's hands and leave them there.

Billy Graham

Snuggle in God's arms. When you are hurting, when you feel lonely or left out, let Him cradle you, comfort you, reassure you of His all-sufficient power and love.

Kay Arthur

We shall find in Christ enough of everything we need— for the body, for the mind, and for the spirit—to do what He wants us to do as long as He wants us to do it.

Vance Havner

How delightful a teacher, but gentle a provider, how bountiful a giver is my Father! Praise, praise to Thee, O manifested Most High.

Jim Elliot

Rejoice always, pray without ceasing, in everything give thanks; for this is the will of God in Christ Jesus for you.

1 Thessalonians 5:16-18 NKJV

Pray Often

Is prayer an integral part of your daily life, or is it a hit-or-miss habit? Do you "pray without ceasing," or is your prayer life an afterthought? Do you regularly pray in the quiet moments of the early morning, or do you bow your head only when others are watching?

As Christians, we are instructed to pray often. But it is important to note that genuine prayer requires much more than bending our knees and closing our eyes. Heartfelt prayer is an attitude of the heart.

If your prayers have become more a matter of habit than a matter of passion, you're robbing yourself of a deeper relationship with God. And how can you rectify this situation? By praying more frequently and more fervently. When you do, God will shower you with His blessings, His grace, and His love.

The quality of your spiritual life will be in direct proportion to the quality of your prayer life: the more you pray, the closer you will feel to God. So today, instead of turning things over in your mind, turn them over to God in prayer. Instead of worrying about your next decision, ask God to lead the way. Don't limit your prayers to the dinner table or the bedside table. Pray constantly about things great and small. God is always listening; it's up to you to do the rest.

God says we don't need to be
anxious about anything;
we just need to pray
about everything.

—

Stormie Omartian

More Great Ideas About Prayer

The center of power is not to be found in summit meetings or in peace conferences. It is not in Peking or Washington or the United Nations, but rather where a child of God prays in the power of the Spirit for God's will to be done in her life, in her home, and in the world around her.

Ruth Bell Graham

What God gives in answer to our prayers will always be the thing we most urgently need, and it will always be sufficient.

Elisabeth Elliot

Learn to pray to God in such a way that you are trusting Him as your Physician to do what He knows is best. Confess to Him the disease, and let Him choose the remedy.

St. Augustine

Those who know God the best are the richest and most powerful in prayer. Little acquaintance with God, and strangeness and coldness to Him, make prayer a rare and feeble thing.

E. M. Bounds

Be an example to the believers in word, in conduct, in love, in spirit, in faith, in purity.

1 Timothy 4:12 NKJV

Being the Right Kind of Example

Whether we like it or not, all of us are role models. Our friends and family members watch our actions and, as followers of Christ, we are obliged to act accordingly.

What kind of example are you? Are you the kind of person whose life serves as a genuine example of righteousness? Are you a person whose behavior serves as a positive role model for others? Are you the kind of person whose actions, day in and day out, are based upon kindness, faithfulness, and a love for the Lord? If so, you are not only blessed by God, but you are also a powerful force for good in a world that desperately needs positive influences such as yours.

We live in a dangerous, temptation-filled world. That's why you encounter so many opportunities to stray from God's commandments. Resist those temptations! When you do, you'll earn God's blessings and you'll serve as a positive role model for your family and friends.

Corrie ten Boom advised, "Don't worry about what you do not understand. Worry about what you do understand in the Bible but do not live by." And that's sound advice because our families and friends are watching . . . and so, for that matter, is God.

More depends on my walk than my talk.

—

D. L. Moody

More Great Ideas About
Setting the Right Kind of Example

In serving we uncover the greatest fulfillment within and become a stellar example of a woman who knows and loves Jesus.

Vonette Bright

Among the most joyful people I have known have been some who seem to have had no human reason for joy. The sweet fragrance of Christ has shown through their lives.

Elisabeth Elliot

You can never separate a leader's actions from his character.

John Maxwell

Integrity of heart is indispensable.

John Calvin

If I take care of my character, my reputation will take care of itself.

D. L. Moody

Heaven and earth will pass away, but My words will never pass away.

Matthew 24:35 HCSB

Trust God's Word

Are you a person who trusts God's Word without reservation? Hopefully so, because the Bible is unlike any other book—it is a guidebook for life here on earth and for life eternal.

As a Christian, you are instructed to study God's Holy Word, to trust His Word, to follow its commandments, and to share its Good News with the world. The Psalmist writes, "Your word is a lamp to my feet and a light to my path" (Psalm 119:105 NASB). Is the Bible your lamp? If not, you are depriving yourself of a priceless gift from the Creator.

Vance Havner observed, "It takes calm, thoughtful, prayerful meditation on the Word to extract its deepest nourishment." How true. God's Word can be a roadmap to a place of righteousness and abundance. Make it your roadmap. God's wisdom can be a light to guide your steps. Claim it as your light today, tomorrow, and every day of your life—and then walk confidently in the footsteps of God's only begotten Son.

More Great Ideas About God's Word

For whatever life holds for you and your family in the coming days, weave the unfailing fabric of God's Word through your heart and mind. It will hold strong, even if the rest of life unravels.

Gigi Graham Tchividjian

Words fail to express my love for this holy Book, my gratitude for its author, for His love and goodness. How shall I thank him for it?

Lottie Moon

I believe the reason so many are failing today is that they have not disciplined themselves to read God's Word consistently, day in and day out, and to apply it to every situation in life.

Kay Arthur

God has given us all sorts of counsel and direction in his written Word; thank God, we have it written down in black and white.

John Eldredge

Meditating upon His Word will inevitably bring peace of mind, strength of purpose, and power for living.

Bill Bright

God can see clearly no matter how dark or foggy the night is. Trust His Word to guide you safely home.

Lisa Whelchel

The promises of Scripture are not mere pious hopes or sanctified guesses. They are more than sentimental words to be printed on decorated cards for Sunday School children. They are eternal verities. They are true. There is no perhaps about them.

Peter Marshall

It takes calm, thoughtful, prayerful meditation on the Word to extract its deepest nourishment.

Vance Havner

The Bible became a living book and a guide for my life.

Vonette Bright

Acquire wisdom—how much better it is than gold! And acquire understanding—it is preferable to silver.

Proverbs 16:16 HCSB

Acquiring Wisdom

Proverbs 16:16 teaches us that wisdom is more valuable than gold. All of us would like to be wise, but not all of us are willing to do the work that is required to become wise. Wisdom is not like a mushroom; it does not spring up overnight. It is, instead, like an oak tree that starts as a tiny acorn, grows into a sapling, and eventually reaches up to the sky, tall and strong.

To become wise, we must seek God's wisdom and live according to His Word. To become wise, we must seek wisdom with consistency and purpose. To become wise, we must not only learn the lessons of the Christian life, we must also live by them.

Do you seek to live a life of righteousness and wisdom? If so, you must study the ultimate source of wisdom: the Word of God. You must seek out worthy mentors and listen carefully to their advice. You must associate, day in and day out, with godly men and women. Then, as you accumulate wisdom, you must not keep it for yourself; you must, instead, share it with your friends and family members.

But be forewarned: if you sincerely seek to share your hard-earned wisdom with others, your actions must give credence to your words. The best way to share one's wisdom—perhaps the only way—is not by words, but by example.

Knowledge is horizontal.
Wisdom is vertical;
it comes down from above.

—

Billy Graham

More Great Ideas About Wisdom

This is my song through endless ages: Jesus led me all the way.

Fanny Crosby

If we neglect the Bible, we cannot expect to benefit from the wisdom and direction that result from knowing God's Word.

Vonette Bright

The more wisdom enters our hearts, the more we will be able to trust our hearts in difficult situations.

John Eldredge

Patience is the companion of wisdom.

St. Augustine

When you and I are related to Jesus Christ, our strength and wisdom and peace and joy and love and hope may run out, but His life rushes in to keep us filled to the brim. We are showered with blessings, not because of anything we have or have not done, but simply because of Him.

Anne Graham Lotz

But the fruit of the Spirit is love, joy, peace, patience, kindness, goodness, faith, gentleness, self-control. Against such things there is no law.

Galatians 5:22-23 HCSB

The Fruit of the Spirit

In Galatians 5, we are also told that when people live by the Spirit, they will bear "fruit of the Spirit." But what, exactly, is the fruit of the Spirit? It's a way of behaving yourself, a way of treating other people, a way of showing the world what it means to be a Christian. The Bible says, "The fruit of the Spirit is love, joy, peace, patience, kindness, goodness, faith, gentleness, self-control."

Today and every day, will you strive to be patient, joyful, loving, and kind? Will you really try to control yourself? And while you're at it, will you be peaceful, gentle, patient, and faithful? If so, you'll demonstrate to the world that the fruit of the Spirit can make a wonderful difference in the lives of good Christian people—people like you!

More Great Ideas About the Fruit of the Spirit

Though we, as Christians, are like Christ, having the first fruits of the Spirit, we are unlike Him, having the remainders of the flesh.

Thomas Watson

The Holy Spirit cannot be located as a guest in a house. He invades everything.

Oswald Chambers

The more we abide in Christ, the more fruit we bear.

Warren Wiersbe

Some people have received Christ but have never reached spiritual maturity. We should grow as Christians every day, and we are not completely mature until we live in the presence of Christ.

Billy Graham

The Holy Spirit is like a living and continually flowing fountain in believers. We have the boundless privilege of tapping into that fountain every time we pray.

Shirley Dobson

When I was a child, I spoke as a child, I understood as a child, I thought as a child; but when I became a man, I put away childish things.

1 Corinthians 13:11 NKJV

Still Growing Up

The journey toward spiritual maturity lasts a lifetime. As Christians, we can and should continue to grow in the love and the knowledge of our Savior as long as we live. Norman Vincent Peale had the following advice for believers of all ages: "Ask the God who made you to keep remaking you." That advice, of course, is perfectly sound, but often ignored.

When we cease to grow, either emotionally or spiritually, we do ourselves a profound disservice. But, if we study God's Word, if we obey His commandments, and if we live in the center of His will, we will not be "stagnant" believers; we will, instead, be growing Christians . . . and that's exactly what God intends for us to be.

Life is a series of choices and decisions. Each day, we make countless decisions that can bring us closer to God . . . or not. When we live according to the principles contained in God's Holy Word, we embark upon a journey of spiritual maturity that results in life abundant and life eternal.

More Great Ideas About Maturity

The disappointment has come, not because God desires to hurt you or make you miserable or to demoralize you, or ruin your life, or keep you from ever knowing happiness. He wants you to be perfect and complete in every aspect, lacking nothing. It's not the easy times that make you more like Jesus, but the hard times.

Kay Arthur

Salvation is the process that's done, that's secure, that no one can take away from you. Sanctification is the lifelong process of being changed from one degree of glory to the next, growing in Christ, putting away the old, taking on the new.

Max Lucado

Growth in depth and strength and consistency and fruitfulness and ultimately in Christlikeness is only possible when the winds of life are contrary to personal comfort.

Anne Graham Lotz

Integrity and maturity are two character traits vital to the heart of a leader.

Charles Stanley

I've never met anyone who became instantly mature. It's a painstaking process that God takes us through, and it includes such things as waiting, failing, losing, and being misunderstood—each calling for extra doses of perseverance.

Charles Swindoll

Being a Christian means accepting the terms of creation, accepting God as our maker and redeemer, and growing day by day into an increasingly glorious creature in Christ, developing joy, experiencing love, maturing in peace.

Eugene Peterson

We cannot hope to reach Christian maturity in any way other than by yielding ourselves utterly and willingly to His mighty working.

Hannah Whitall Smith

When I was young I was sure of everything; in a few years, having been mistaken a thousand times, I was not half so sure of most things as I was before; at present, I am hardly sure of anything but what God has revealed to me.

John Wesley

Shepherd God's flock among you, not overseeing out of compulsion but freely, according to God's will; not for the money but eagerly.

1 Peter 5:2 HCSB

Christ-Centered Leadership

The old saying is familiar and true: imitation is the sincerest form of flattery. As believers, we are called to imitate, as best we can, the carpenter from Galilee. The task of imitating Christ is often difficult and sometimes impossible, but as Christians, we must continue to try.

Our world needs leaders who willingly honor Christ with their words and their deeds, but not necessarily in that order. If you seek to be such a leader, then you must begin by making yourself a worthy example to your family, to your friends, to your church, and to your community. After all, your words of instruction will never ring true unless you yourself are willing to follow them.

Christ-centered leadership is an exercise in service: service to God in heaven and service to His children here on earth. Christ willingly became a servant to His followers, and you must seek to do the same for yours.

Are you the kind of servant-leader whom you would want to follow? If so, congratulations: you are honoring your Savior by imitating Him. And that, of course, is the sincerest form of flattery.

More Great Ideas About Leadership

A man ought to live so that everybody knows he is a Christian, and most of all, his family ought to know.

D. L. Moody

A wise leader chooses a variety of gifted individuals. He complements his strengths.

Charles Stanley

A true and safe leader is likely to be one who has not desire to lead, but is forced into a position of leadership by inward pressure of the Holy Spirit and the press of external situation.

A. W. Tozer

You can never separate a leader's actions from his character.

John Maxwell

All bitterness, anger and wrath, insult and slander must be removed from you, along with all wickedness. And be kind and compassionate to one another, forgiving one another, just as God also forgave you in Christ.

Ephesians 4:31-32 HCSB

Beyond Bitterness

In the fourth chapter of Ephesians, we are warned about the dangers of bitterness, and with good reason. Bitterness is a spiritual sickness. It will consume your soul; it is dangerous to your emotional health. It can destroy you if you let it . . . so don't let it!

If you are caught up in intense feelings of anger or resentment, you know all too well the destructive power of these emotions. How can you rid yourself of these feelings? First, you must prayerfully ask God to cleanse your heart. Then, you must learn to catch yourself whenever thoughts of bitterness or hatred begin to attack you. Your challenge is this: You must learn to resist negative thoughts before they hijack your emotions.

When you learn to direct your thoughts toward more positive (and rational) topics, you'll be protected from the spiritual and emotional consequences of bitterness . . . and you'll be wiser, healthier, and happier, too. So why wait? Defeat destructive bitterness today.

More Great Ideas About Bitterness

Bitterness is a spiritual cancer, a rapidly growing malignancy that can consume your life. Bitterness cannot be ignored but must be healed at the very core, and only Christ can heal bitterness.

Beth Moore

Sin is any deed or memory that hampers or binds human personality.

Catherine Marshall

Forgiveness enables you to bury your grudge in icy earth. To put the past behind you. To flush resentment away by being the first to forgive. Forgiveness fashions your future. It is a brave and brash thing to do.

Barbara Johnson

Grudges are like hand grenades; it is wise to release them before they destroy you.

Barbara Johnson

Bitterness is the trap that snares the hunter.

Max Lucado

A heart out of tune, out of sync with God's heart, will produce a life of spiritual barrenness and missed opportunities.

Jim Cymbala

Forgiveness is the key that unlocks the door of resentment and the handcuffs of hate. It is a power that breaks the chains of bitterness and the shackles of selfishness.

Corrie ten Boom

Bitterness only makes suffering worse and closes the spiritual channels through which God can pour His grace.

Warren Wiersbe

Bitterness is the greatest barrier to friendship with God.

Rick Warren

Be patient and understanding. Life is too short to be vengeful or malicious.

Phillips Brooks

*Be strong and courageous, and do the work. Do not be afraid
or discouraged, for the Lord God, my God, is with you.*

1 Chronicles 28:20 NIV

Beyond the Fear of Failure

As we consider the uncertainties of the future, we are confronted with a powerful temptation: the temptation to "play it safe." Unwilling to move mountains, we fret over molehills. Unwilling to entertain great hopes for tomorrow, we focus on the unfairness of today. Unwilling to trust God completely, we take timid half-steps when God intends that we make giant leaps.

Today, ask God for the courage to step beyond the boundaries of your doubts. Ask Him to guide you to a place where you can realize your full potential—a place where you are freed from the fear of failure. Ask Him to do His part, and promise Him that you will do your part. Don't ask Him to lead you to a "safe" place; ask Him to lead you to the "right" place . . . and remember: those two places are seldom the same.

More Great Ideas About
Fear of Failure

With each new experience of letting God be in control, we gain courage and reinforcement for daring to do it again and again.

Gloria Gaither

Risk must be taken because the greatest hazard in life is to risk nothing.

John Maxwell

Only a person who dares to risk is free.

Joey Johnson

There comes a time when we simply have to face the challenges in our lives and stop backing down.

John Eldredge

Do not be one of those who, rather than risk failure, never attempt anything.

Thomas Merton

One thing I do, forgetting those things which are behind and reaching forward to those things which are ahead, I press toward the goal for the prize of the upward call of God in Christ Jesus.

Philippians 3:13-14 NKJV

Making Peace with Your Past

Because you are human, you may be slow to forget yesterday's disappointments. But, if you sincerely seek to focus your hopes and energies on the future, then you must find ways to accept the past, no matter how difficult it may be to do so.

In the third chapter of Philippians, Paul tells us that he chose to focus on the future, not the past. Have you made peace with your past? If so, congratulations. But, if you are mired in the quicksand of regret, it's time to plan your escape. How can you do so? By accepting what has been and by trusting God for what will be.

So, if you have not yet made peace with the past, today is the day to declare an end to all hostilities. When you do, you can then turn your thoughts to the wondrous promises of God and to the glorious future that He has in store for you.

More Great Ideas About the Past

Yesterday is just experience but tomorrow is glistening with purpose—and today is the channel leading from one to the other.

Barbara Johnson

Every time the devil reminds you of your past . . . remind him of his future—and yours!

Anonymous

We set our eyes on the finish line, forgetting the past, and straining toward the mark of spiritual maturity and fruitfulness.

Vonette Bright

We can't just put our pasts behind us. We've got to put our pasts in front of God.

Beth Moore

Yesterday ended last night.

John Maxwell

Whoever you are, whatever your condition or circumstance, whatever your past or problem, Jesus can restore you to wholeness.

Anne Graham Lotz

The pages of your past cannot be rewritten, but the pages of your tomorrows are blank.

Zig Ziglar

Our yesterdays present irreparable things to us; it is true that we have lost opportunities which will never return, but God can transform this destructive anxiety into a constructive thoughtfulness for the future. Let the past sleep, but let it sleep on the bosom of Christ. Leave the Irreparable Past in His hands, and step out into the Irresistible Future with Him.

Oswald Chambers

The wise man gives proper appreciation in his life to his past. He learns to sift the sawdust of heritage in order to find the nuggets that make the current moment have any meaning.

Grady Nutt

Therefore, get your minds ready for action, being self-disciplined, and set your hope completely on the grace to be brought to you at the revelation of Jesus Christ.

1 Peter 1:13 HCSB

The Need for Self-Discipline

God's Word reminds us again and again that our Creator expects us to lead disciplined lives. God doesn't reward laziness, misbehavior, or apathy. To the contrary, He expects us to behave with dignity and discipline. But ours is a world in which dignity and discipline are often in short supply.

We live in a world in which leisure is glorified and indifference is often glamorized. But God has other plans. God gives us talents, and He expects us to use them. But it is not always easy to cultivate those talents. Sometimes, we must invest countless hours (or, in some cases, many years) honing our skills. And that's perfectly okay with God, because He understands that self-discipline is a blessing, not a burden.

Proverbs 23:12 advises: "Apply your heart to discipline And your ears to words of knowledge" (NASB). And, 2 Peter 1:5-6 teaches, "make every effort to supplement your faith with goodness, goodness with knowledge, knowledge with self-control, self-control with endurance, endurance with godliness" (HCSB). Thus, God's Word is clear: we must exercise self-discipline in all matters.

When we pause to consider how much work needs to be done, we realize that self-discipline is not simply a proven way to get ahead, it's also an integral part of God's plan for our lives. If we genuinely seek to be faithful stewards of our time, our talents, and our resources, we must adopt a disciplined approach to life. Otherwise, our talents are wasted and our resources are squandered.

Life's greatest rewards seldom fall into our laps; to the contrary, our greatest accomplishments usually require work, perseverance, and discipline. May we, as disciplined believers, be willing to work for the rewards we so earnestly desire.

> Discipline is training that develops and corrects.
>
> —
>
> *Charles Stanley*

More from God's Word

Obedience to God is our job. The results of that obedience are God's.

Elisabeth Elliot

"They that sow bountifully shall reap also bountifully," is as true in spiritual things as in material.

Lottie Moon

Hoping for a good future without investing in today is like a farmer waiting for a crop without ever planting any seed.

John Maxwell

The effective Christians of history have been men and women of great personal discipline—mental discipline, discipline of the body, discipline of the tongue, and discipline of the emotion.

Billy Graham

You can't climb the ladder of life with your hands in your pockets.

Barbara Johnson

But when the Helper comes, whom I shall send to you from the Father, the Spirit of truth who proceeds from the Father, He will testify of Me.

John 15:26 NKJV

Filled with the Holy Spirit

Are you burdened by the pressures of everyday living? If so, it's time to ease the pressure. How can you do it? By allowing the Holy Spirit to fill you and to do His work in your life.

When you are filled with the Holy Spirit, your words and deeds will reflect a love and devotion to God. When you are filled with the Holy Spirit, the steps of your life's journey are guided by the Creator of the universe. When you allow God's Spirit to work in you and through you, you will be energized and transformed.

So today, take God at His word. He has promised to fill you with His Spirit if you let Him. Let Him. And then stand back in amazement as the Father begins to work miracles in your own life and in the lives of those you love.

More Great Ideas About
the Holy Spirit

The Holy Spirit will not come to us in his fullness until we see and assent to his priority—his passion for ministry.

Catherine Marshall

The church needs the power and the gifts of the Holy Spirit more now than ever before.

Corrie ten Boom

The Christian is never to be out of the control of the Holy Spirit.

Kay Arthur

It is the primary responsibility of the Holy Spirit to glorify Jesus by making us like Him—in our character, in our commitment, and in our communion with the Father.

Anne Graham Lotz

Father, for this day, renew within me the gift of the Holy Spirit.

Andrew Murray

The Lord Jesus by His Holy Spirit is with me, and the knowledge of His presence dispels the darkness and allays any fears.

Bill Bright

I can usually sense that a leading is from the Holy Spirit when it calls me to humble myself, to serve somebody, to encourage somebody, or to give something away. Very rarely will the evil one lead us to do those kind of things.

Bill Hybels

God wants to teach us that when we commit our lives to Him, He gives us that wonderful teacher, the Holy Spirit.

Gloria Gaither

We have given too much attention to methods and to machinery and to resources, and too little to the Source of Power, the filling with the Holy Ghost.

J. Hudson Taylor

Before we can be filled with the Spirit, the desire to be filled must be all-consuming. It must be the biggest thing in the life, so acute, so intrusive as to crowd out everything else.

A. W. Tozer

So he who had received five talents came and brought five other talents, saying, "Lord, you delivered to me five talents; look, I have gained five more talents besides them." His lord said to him, "Well done, good and faithful servant; you were faithful over a few things, I will make you ruler over many things. Enter into the joy of your lord."

Matthew 25:20-21 NKJV

Using Your Talents

The old saying is both familiar and true: "What we are is God's gift to us; what we become is our gift to God." Each of us possesses special talents, gifted by God, that can be nurtured carefully or ignored totally. Our challenge, of course, is to use our abilities to the greatest extent possible and to use them in ways that honor our Savior.

Are you using your natural talents to make God's world a better place? If so, congratulations. But if you have gifts that you have not fully explored and developed, perhaps you need to have a chat with the One who gave you those gifts in the first place. Your talents are priceless treasures offered from your Heavenly Father. Use them. After all, an obvious way to say "thank you" to the Giver is to use the gifts He has given.

More Great Ideas About Talents

In the great orchestra we call life, you have an instrument and a song, and you owe it to God to play them both sublimely.

Max Lucado

God often reveals His direction for our lives through the way He made us . . . with a certain personality and unique skills.

Bill Hybels

Not everyone possesses boundless energy or a conspicuous talent. We are not equally blessed with great intellect or physical beauty or emotional strength. But we have all been given the same ability to be faithful.

Gigi Graham Tchividjian

One thing taught large in the Holy Scriptures is that while God gives His gifts freely, He will require a strict accounting of them at the end of the road. Each man is personally responsible for his store, be it large or small, and will be required to explain his use of it before the judgment seat of Christ.

A. W. Tozer

The Lord is glad to open the gate to every knocking soul. It opens very freely; its hinges are not rusted, no bolts secure it. Have faith and enter at this moment through holy courage. If you knock with a heavy heart, you shall yet sing with joy of spirit. Never be discouraged!

C. H. Spurgeon

God has given you special talents—now it's your turn to give them back to God.

Marie T. Freeman

You are a unique blend of talents, skills, and gifts, which makes you an indispensable member of the body of Christ.

Charles Stanley

What we are is God's gift to us. What we become is our gift to God.

Anonymous

You are the only person on earth who can use your ability.

Zig Ziglar

Pride goes before destruction, and a haughty spirit before a fall.

Proverbs 16:18 NKJV

Beware of Pride

The words from Proverbs 16 remind us that pride and destruction are traveling partners. But as imperfect human beings, we are tempted to puff out our chests and crow about our own accomplishments. When we do so, we delude ourselves.

As Christians, we have a profound reason to be humble: We have been refashioned and saved by Jesus Christ, and that salvation came not because of our own good works but because of God's love and His grace. Thus, we are not self-made men and women; we are "God-made" and "Christ-saved." How, then, can we be boastful? The answer, of course, is simple: if we are honest with ourselves and with our God, we cannot be boastful. In the quiet moments, when we search the depths of our own hearts, we know that whatever "it" is, God did that. And He deserves the credit.

More Great Ideas About Pride

We cannot be filled until we are empty. We have to be poor in spirit of ourselves in order to be filled with the Holy Spirit.

Corrie ten Boom

All kindness and good deeds, we must keep silent. The result will be an inner reservoir of personality power.

Catherine Marshall

Our Lord did not say it was wrong to pray in the corners of the street, but he did say it was wrong to have the motive to "be seen of men."

Oswald Chambers

When you have good, healthy relationships with your family and friends you're more prompted to laugh and not take yourself so seriously.

Dennis Swanberg

Pride has a devilish quality that keeps us from sensing our need for God's grace.

Jim Cymbala

It was as important to me that my children be no more self-righteous than they were unrighteous. In His Gospels, Christ seemed far more tolerant of a repentant sinner than a self-righteous, self-proclaimed saint.

Beth Moore

There is nothing so natural to man, nothing so insidious and hidden from our sight, nothing so difficult and dangerous, as pride.

Andrew Murray

Jesus had a humble heart. If He abides in us, pride will never dominate our lives.

Billy Graham

That's what I love about serving God. In His eyes, there are no little people . . . because there are no big people. We are all on the same playing field. We all start at square one. No one has it better than the other, or possesses unfair advantage.

Joni Eareckson Tada

Humility is a thing which must be genuine; the imitation of it is the nearest thing in the world to pride.

C. H. Spurgeon

If we confess our sins, He is faithful and righteous to forgive us our sins and to cleanse us from all unrighteousness.

1 John 1:9 HCSB

Real Repentance

Who among us has sinned? All of us. But, God calls upon us to turn away from sin by following His commandments. And the good news is this: When we do ask God's forgiveness and turn our hearts to Him, He forgives us absolutely and completely.

Genuine repentance requires more than simply offering God apologies for our misdeeds. Real repentance may start with feelings of sorrow and remorse, but it ends only when we turn away from the sin that has heretofore distanced us from our Creator. In truth, we offer our most meaningful apologies to God, not with our words, but with our actions. As long as we are still engaged in sin, we may be "repenting," but we have not fully "repented."

Is there an aspect of your life that is distancing you from your God? If so, ask for His forgiveness, and—just as importantly—stop sinning. Then, wrap yourself in the protection of God's Word. When you do, you will be secure.

More Great Ideas About Repentance

God sees everything we've ever done and He's willing to forgive. But we must confess to him.

Ruth Bell Graham

Full and true repentance is literally an about-face. It means turning completely around, away from sin, and turning toward God.

Shirley Dobson

Real repentance is always accompanied by godly sorrow. Asking God to forgive us for a sin we are not yet sorry we committed is a waste of time.

Beth Moore

Four marks of true repentance are: acknowledgement of wrong, willingness to confess it, willingness to abandon it, and willingness to make restitution.

Corrie ten Boom

Repentance is an inward conviction that expresses itself in an outward action.

Max Lucado

In terms of the parable of the Prodigal Son, repentance is the flight home that leads to joyful celebration. It opens the way to a future, to a relationship restored.

Philip Yancey

We have a decision to make—to turn away from sin or to be miserable and suffer the consequences of continual disobedience.

Vonette Bright

Repentance is among other things a sincere apology to God for distrusting Him so long, and faith is throwing oneself upon Christ in complete confidence.

A. W. Tozer

The pardon of God deletes past, present, and future sins—completely!

Franklin Graham

Repentance involves a radical change of heart and mind in which we agree with God's evaluation of our sin and then take specific action to align ourselves with His will.

Henry Blackaby

For if you forgive people their wrongdoing, your heavenly Father will forgive you as well. But if you don't forgive people, your Father will not forgive your wrongdoing.

Matthew 6:14-15 HCSB

Forgiveness Now

Forgiving other people is hard—sometimes very hard. But God tells us that we must forgive others, even when we'd rather not. So, if you're angry with anybody (or if you're upset by something you yourself have done), it's time to forgive . . . now!

Life would be much simpler if you could forgive people "once and for all" and be done with it. Yet forgiveness is seldom that easy. Usually, the decision to forgive is straightforward, but the process of forgiving is more difficult. Forgiveness is a journey that requires effort, time, perseverance, and prayer.

God instructs you to treat other people exactly as you wish to be treated. And since you want to be forgiven for the mistakes that you make, you must be willing to extend forgiveness to other people for the mistakes that they have made. If you can't seem to forgive someone, you should keep asking God to help you until you do. And you can be sure of this: if you keep asking for God's help, He will give it.

More Great Ideas About Forgiveness

Only the truly forgiven are truly forgiving.

C. S. Lewis

Our relationships with other people are of primary importance to God. Because God is love, He cannot tolerate any unforgiveness or hardness in us toward any individual.

Catherine Marshall

Revenge is the raging fire that consumes the arsonist.

Max Lucado

As you have received the mercy of God by the forgiveness of sin and the promise of eternal life, thus you must show mercy.

Billy Graham

I firmly believe a great many prayers are not answered because we are not willing to forgive someone.

D. L. Moody

It is better to forgive and forget than to resent and remember.

Barbara Johnson

Forgiveness is not an emotion. Forgiveness is an act of the will, and the will can function regardless of the temperature of the heart.

Corrie ten Boom

The more you practice the art of forgiving, the quicker you'll master the art of living.

Marie T. Freeman

Our forgiveness toward others should flow from a realization and appreciation of God's forgiveness toward us.

Franklin Graham

To hold on to hate and resentments is to throw a monkey wrench into the machinery of life.

E. Stanley Jones

Don't be deceived: God is not mocked. For whatever a man sows he will also reap, because the one who sows to his flesh will reap corruption from the flesh, but the one who sows to the Spirit will reap eternal life from the Spirit.

Galatians 6:7-8 HCSB

Choose Wisely

Life is a series of choices. Each day, we make countless decisions that can bring us closer to God… or not. When we live according to God's commandments, we earn for ourselves the abundance and peace that He intends for our lives. But, when we turn our backs upon God by disobeying Him, we bring needless suffering upon ourselves and our families.

Do you seek God's peace and His blessings? Then obey Him. When you're faced with a difficult choice or a powerful temptation, seek God's counsel and trust the counsel He gives. Invite God into your heart and live according to His commandments. When you do, you will be blessed today, and tomorrow, and forever.

More Great Ideas About Behavior

Our response to God determines His response to us.

Henry Blackaby

When you discover the Christian way, you discover your own way as a person.

E. Stanley Jones

Don't worry about what you do not understand. Worry about what you do understand in the Bible but do not live by.

Corrie ten Boom

There may be no trumpet sound or loud applause when we make a right decision, just a calm sense of resolution and peace.

Gloria Gaither

Christianity says we were created by a righteous God to flourish and be exhilarated in a righteous environment. God has "wired" us in such a way that the more righteous we are, the more we'll actually enjoy life.

Bill Hybels

Be anxious for nothing, but in everything by prayer and supplication, with thanksgiving, let your requests be made known to God.

Philippians 4:6 NKJV

Beyond Anxiety

We live in a world that often breeds anxiety and fear. When we come face to face with tough times, we may fall prey to discouragement, doubt, or depression. But our Father in Heaven has other plans. God has promised that we may lead lives of abundance, not anxiety. In fact, His Word instructs us to "be anxious for nothing." But how can we put our fears to rest? By taking those fears to God and leaving them there.

As you face the challenges of everyday living, do you find yourself becoming anxious, troubled, discouraged, or fearful? If so, turn every one of your concerns over to your Heavenly Father. The same God who created the universe will comfort you if you ask Him…so ask Him and trust Him. And then watch in amazement as your anxieties melt into the warmth of His loving hands.

More Great Ideas About Anxiety

So often we pray and then fret anxiously, waiting for God to hurry up and do something. All the while God is waiting for us to calm down, so He can do something through us.

Corrie ten Boom

Worry and anxiety are sand in the machinery of life; faith is the oil.

E. Stanley Jones

The fierce grip of panic need not immobilize you. God knows no limitation when it comes to deliverance. Admit your fear. Commit it to Him. Dump the pressure on Him. He can handle it.

Charles Swindoll

Some people feel guilty about their anxieties and regard them as a defect of faith, but they are afflictions, not sins. Like all afflictions, they are, if we can so take them, our share in the passion of Christ.

C. S. Lewis

We must lay our questions, frustrations, anxieties, and impotence at the feet of God and wait for His answer. And then receiving it, we must live by faith.

Kay Arthur

Draw near to God, and He will draw near to you.

James 4:8 HCSB

Draw Near to God

If God is everywhere, why does He sometimes seem so far away? The answer to that question, of course, has nothing to do with God and everything to do with us.

When we begin each day on our knees, in praise and worship to Him, God often seems very near indeed. But, if we ignore God's presence or—worse yet—rebel against it altogether, the world in which we live becomes a spiritual wasteland.

Are you tired, discouraged, or fearful? Be comforted because God is with you. Are you confused? Listen to the quiet voice of your Heavenly Father. Are you bitter? Talk with God and seek His guidance. Are you celebrating a great victory? Thank God and praise Him. He is the Giver of all things good.

In whatever condition you find yourself, wherever you are, whether you are happy or sad, victorious or vanquished, troubled or triumphant, celebrate God's presence. And be comforted. God is not just near; He has promised that He is right here, right now. And that's a promise you can depend on.

More Great Ideas About God's Presence

If you want to hear God's voice clearly and you are uncertain, then remain in His presence until He changes that uncertainty. Often, much can happen during this waiting for the Lord. Sometimes, He changes pride into humility, doubt into faith and peace.

Corrie ten Boom

If your heart has grown cold, it is because you have moved away from the fire of His presence.

Beth Moore

God walks with us. He scoops us up in His arms or simply sits with us in silent strength until we cannot avoid the awesome recognition that yes, even now, He is here.

Gloria Gaither

As God perfects us, He keeps us protected from the pride that might otherwise develop by veiling, to some extent, our progress in our own eyes. The light of the glory of His presence shines two ways: it sheds light on the knowledge of God so that we can learn to see Him more clearly, but it also sheds light on ourselves so that we can see our own sin more clearly.

Beth Moore

There is a basic urge: the longing for unity. You desire a reunion with God—with God your Father.

E. Stanley Jones

God does not dispense strength and encouragement like a druggist fills your prescription. The Lord doesn't promise to give us something to take so we can handle our weary moments. He promises us Himself. That is all. And that is enough.

Charles Swindoll

Make the least of all that goes and the most of all that comes. Don't regret what is past. Cherish what you have. Look forward to all that is to come. And most important of all, rely moment by moment on Jesus Christ.

Gigi Graham Tchividjian

A sense of deity is inscribed on every heart.

John Calvin

Get into the habit of dealing with God about everything. Unless, in the first waking moment of the day you learn to fling the door wide back and let God in, you will work on a wrong level all day. But, swing the door wide open and pray to your Father in secret, and every public thing will be stamped with the presence of God.

Oswald Chambers

He awakens Me morning by morning, He awakens My ear to hear as the learned. The Lord God has opened My ear.

Isaiah 50:4-5 NKJV

How to Start the Day

Each new day is a gift from God, and if we are wise, we spend a few quiet moments each morning thanking the Giver. Daily life is woven together with the threads of habit, and no habit is more important to our spiritual health than the discipline of daily prayer and devotion to the Creator.

When we begin each day with heads bowed and hearts lifted, we remind ourselves of God's love, His protection, and His commandments. And if we are wise, we align our priorities for the coming day with the teachings and commandments that God has given us through His Holy Word.

Are you seeking to change some aspect of your life? Do you seek to improve the condition of your spiritual or physical health? If so, ask for God's help and ask for it many times each day . . . starting with your morning devotional.

More Great Ideas About
Daily Devotions

Think of this—we may live together with Him here and now, a daily walking with Him who loved us and gave Himself for us.

Elisabeth Elliot

I believe the reason so many are failing today is that they have not disciplined themselves to read God's Word consistently, day in and day out, and to apply it to every situation in life.

Kay Arthur

Knowing God involves an intimate, personal relationship that is developed over time through prayer and getting answers to prayer, through Bible study and applying its teaching to our lives, through obedience and experiencing the power of God, through moment-by-moment submission to Him that results in a moment-by-moment filling of the Holy Spirit.

Anne Graham Lotz

Our devotion to God is strengthened when we offer Him a fresh commitment each day.

Elizabeth George

How motivating it has been for me to view my early morning devotions as time of retreat alone with Jesus, Who desires that I "come with Him by myself to a quiet place" in order to pray, read His Word, listen for His voice, and be renewed in my spirit.

Anne Graham Lotz

There is no way to draw closer to God unless you are in the Word of God every day. It's your compass. Your guide. You can't get where you need to go without it.

Stormie Omartian

God is a place of safety you can run to, but it helps if you are running to Him on a daily basis so that you are in familiar territory.

Stormie Omartian

We must appropriate the tender mercy of God every day after conversion or problems quickly develop. We need his grace daily in order to live a righteous life.

Jim Cymbala

We are hard pressed on every side, yet not crushed; we are perplexed, but not in despair.

2 Corinthians 4:8 NKJV

Beyond Discouragement

We Christians have many reasons to celebrate. God is in His heaven; Christ has risen, and we are the sheep of His flock. Yet sometimes, even the most devout believers may become discouraged. After all, we live in a world where expectations can be high and demands can be even higher.

When we fail to meet the expectations of others (or, for that matter, the expectations that we have for ourselves), we may be tempted to abandon hope. But God has other plans. He knows exactly how He intends to use us. Our task is to remain faithful until He does.

If you become discouraged with the direction of your day or your life, turn your thoughts and prayers to God. He is a God of possibility, not negativity. He will help you count your blessings instead of your hardships. And then, with a renewed spirit of optimism and hope, you can properly thank your Father in heaven for His blessings, for His love, and for His Son.

More Great Ideas About Disappointments

If your hopes are being disappointed just now, it means that they are being purified.

Oswald Chambers

Though our pain and our disappointment and the details of our suffering may differ, there is an abundance of God's grace and peace available to each of us.

Charles Swindoll

The next time you're disappointed, don't panic and don't give up. Just be patient and let God remind you he's still in control.

Max Lucado

Why should I ever resist any delay or disappointment, any affliction or oppression or humiliation, when I know God will use it in my life to make me like Jesus and to prepare me for heaven?

Kay Arthur

Often God has to shut a door in our face so that he can subsequently open the door through which he wants us to go.

Catherine Marshall

The difference between winning and losing is how we choose to react to disappointment.

—

Barbara Johnson

Let not your heart be troubled: ye believe in God, believe also in me. In my Father's house are many mansions: if it were not so, I would have told you. I go to prepare a place for you. And if I go and prepare a place for you, I will come again, and receive you unto myself; that where I am, there ye may be also.

John 14:1-3 KJV

This World Is Not Your Home

Sometimes life's inevitable troubles and heartbreaks are easier to tolerate when we remind ourselves that heaven is our true home. An old hymn contains the words, "This world is not my home; I'm just passing through." Thank goodness!

For believers, death is not an ending; it is a beginning. For believers, the grave is not a final resting-place; it is a place of transition. Death can never claim those who have accepted Christ as their personal Savior. Christ has promised that He has gone to prepare a glorious home in heaven—a timeless, blessed gift to His children—and Jesus always keeps His promises.

If you've committed your life to Christ, your time here on earth is merely a preparation for a far different life to come: your eternal life with Jesus and a host of fellow believers.

So, while this world can be a place of temporary hardship and temporary suffering, you can be comforted in the knowledge that God offers you a permanent home that is free from all suffering and pain. Please take God at His word. When you do, you can withstand any problem, knowing that your troubles are temporary, but that heaven is not.

More Great Ideas About Heaven

Ultimate healing and the glorification of the body are certainly among the blessings of Calvary for the believing Christian. Immediate healing is not guaranteed.

Warren Wiersbe

Exercise and physical fitness have a cause-and-effect relationship; fitness comes as a direct result of regular, sustained, and intense exercise.

John Maxwell

A Christian should no more defile his body than a Jew would defile the temple.

Warren Wiersbe

Therefore, submit to God. But resist the Devil, and he will flee from you. Draw near to God, and He will draw near to you. Cleanse your hands, sinners, and purify your hearts, double-minded people!

James 4:7-8 HCSB

Beware of the Adversary

This world is God's creation, and it contains the wonderful fruits of His handiwork. But, the world also contains countless opportunities to stray from God's will. Temptations are everywhere, and the devil, it seems, never takes a day off. Our task, as believers, is to turn away from temptation and to place our lives squarely in the center of God's will.

In his letter to Jewish Christians, Peter offered a stern warning: "Your adversary, the devil, prowls around like a roaring lion, seeking someone to devour" (1 Peter 5:8 NASB). What was true in New Testament times is equally true in our own. Evil is indeed abroad in the world, and Satan continues to sow the seeds of destruction far and wide. As Christians, we must guard our hearts by earnestly wrapping ourselves in the protection of God's Holy Word. When we do, we are protected.

More Great Ideas About Evil

Christianity isn't a religion about going to Sunday school, potluck suppers, being nice, holding car washes, sending your secondhand clothes off to Mexico—as good as those things might be. This is a world at war.

John Eldredge

The descent to hell is easy, and those who begin by worshipping power soon worship evil.

C. S. Lewis

God loves you, and He yearns for you to turn away from the path of evil. You need His forgiveness, and you need Him to come into your life and remake you from within.

Billy Graham

There is nothing evil in matter itself. Evil lies in the spirit. Evils of the heart, of the mind, of the soul, of the spirit—these have to do with man's sin, and the only reason the human body does evil is because the human spirit uses it to do evil.

A. W. Tozer

Of two evils, choose neither.

C. H. Spurgeon

For I know the thoughts that I think toward you, says the Lord, thoughts of peace and not of evil, to give you a future and a hope. Then you will call upon Me and go and pray to Me, and I will listen to you.

Jeremiah 29:11-12 NKJV

Your Very Bright Future

Because we are saved by a risen Christ, we can have hope for the future, no matter how troublesome our present circumstances may seem. After all, God has promised that we are His throughout eternity. And, He has told us that we must place our hopes in Him.

Of course, we will face disappointments and failures while we are here on earth, but these are only temporary defeats. This world can be a place of trials and tribulations, but when we place our trust in the Giver of all things good, we are secure. God has promised us peace, joy, and eternal life. And God keeps His promises today, tomorrow, and forever.

Are you willing to place your future in the hands of a loving and all-knowing God? Do you trust in the ultimate goodness of His plan for your life? Will you face today's challenges with optimism and hope? You should.

After all, God created you for a very important purpose: His purpose. And you still have important work to do: His work.

Today, as you live in the present and look to the future, remember that God has a plan for you. Act—and believe—accordingly.

Take courage. We walk
in the wilderness today and
in the Promised Land tomorrow.

—

D. L. Moody

More Great Ideas About the Future

The future lies all before us. Shall it only be a slight advance upon what we usually do? Ought it not to be a bound, a leap forward to altitudes of endeavor and success undreamed of before?

Annie Armstrong

The Christian believes in a fabulous future.

Billy Graham

You can look forward with hope, because one day there will be no more separation, no more scars, and no more suffering in My Father's House. It's the home of your dreams!

Anne Graham Lotz

Our future may look fearfully intimidating, yet we can look up to the Engineer of the Universe, confident that nothing escapes His attention or slips out of the control of those strong hands.

Elisabeth Elliot

Allow your dreams a place in your prayers and plans. God-given dreams can help you move into the future He is preparing for you.

Barbara Johnson

In all your ways acknowledge Him, and He shall direct your paths.

Proverbs 3:6 NKJV

Seeking God's Guidance

When we genuinely seek to know the heart of God—when we prayerfully seek His wisdom and His will—our Heavenly Father carefully guides us over the peaks and valleys of life. And as Christians, we can be comforted: Whether we find ourselves at the pinnacle of the mountain or the darkest depths of the valley, the loving heart of God is always there with us.

As Christians whose salvation has been purchased by the blood of Christ, we have every reason to live joyously and courageously. After all, Christ has already fought and won our battle for us—He did so on the cross at Calvary. But despite Christ's sacrifice, and despite God's promises, we may become confused or disoriented by the endless complications and countless distractions of daily life.

If you're unsure of your next step, lean upon God's promises and lift your prayers to Him. Remember that God is always near; remember that He is your protector and your deliverer. Open yourself to His heart, and trust Him to guide your path. When you do, God will direct your steps, and you will receive His blessings today, tomorrow, and throughout eternity.

More Great Ideas About God's Guidance

If we want to hear God's voice, we must surrender our minds and hearts to Him.

Billy Graham

Walk in the daylight of God's will because then you will be safe; you will not stumble.

Anne Graham Lotz

Enjoy the adventure of receiving God guidance. Taste it, revel in it, appreciate the fact that the journey is often a lot more exciting than arriving at the destination.

Bill Hybels

Are you serious about wanting God's guidance to become a personal reality in your life? The first step is to tell God that you know you can't manage your own life; that you need his help.

Catherine Marshall

A man's heart plans his way, but the Lord directs his steps.

Proverbs 16:9 NKJV

His Plans for You

God has a plan for your life. He understands that plan as thoroughly and completely as He knows you. And, if you seek God's will earnestly and prayerfully, He will make His plans known to you in His own time and in His own way.

If you sincerely seek to live in accordance with God's will for your life, you will live in accordance with His commandments. You will study God's Word, and you will be watchful for His signs.

Sometimes, God's plans seem unmistakably clear to you. But other times, He may lead you through the wilderness before He directs you to the Promised Land. So be patient and keep seeking His will for your life. When you do, you'll be amazed at the marvelous things that an all-powerful, all-knowing God can do.

More Great Ideas About God's Plan

God has a plan for the life of every Christian. Every circumstance, every turn of destiny, all things work together for your good and for His glory.

Billy Graham

If not a sparrow falls upon the ground without your Father, you have reason to see that the smallest events of your career and your life are arranged by him.

C. H. Spurgeon

God has a course mapped out for your life, and all the inadequacies in the world will not change His mind. He will be with you every step of the way. And though it may take time, He has a celebration planned for when you cross over the "Red Seas" of your life.

Charles Swindoll

If you believe in a God who controls the big things, you have to believe in a God who controls the little things. It is we, of course, to whom things look "little" or "big."

Elisabeth Elliot

It's incredible to realize that what we do each day has meaning in the big picture of God's plan.

Bill Hybels

I don't doubt that the Holy Spirit guides your decisions from within when you make them with the intention of pleasing God. The error would be to think that He speaks only within, whereas in reality He speaks also through Scripture, the Church, Christian friends, and books.

C. S. Lewis

Our heavenly Father never takes anything from his children unless he means to give them something better.

George Mueller

I thought God's purpose was to make me full of happiness and joy. It is, but it is happiness and joy from God's standpoint, not from mine.

Oswald Chambers

God's goal is not to make you happy. It is to make you his.

Max Lucado

Can you understand the secrets of God? His limits are higher than the heavens; you cannot reach them! They are deeper than the grave; you cannot understand them! His limits are longer than the earth and wider than the sea.

Job 11:7-9 NCV

He Reigns

God is sovereign. He reigns over the entire universe and He reigns over your little corner of that universe. Your challenge is to recognize God's sovereignty, to live in accordance with His commandments, and to trust His promises. Sometimes, of course, these tasks are easier said than done.

Your Heavenly Father may not always reveal Himself as quickly (or as clearly) as you would like. But rest assured: God is in control, God is here, and God intends to use you in wonderful, unexpected ways. He desires to lead you along a path of His choosing. Your challenge is to watch, to listen, to learn . . . and to follow. Today.

More Great Ideas About God's Sovereignty

We do not understand the intricate pattern of the stars in their course, but we know that He Who created them does, and that just as surely as He guides them, He is charting a safe course for us.

Billy Graham

Every experience God gives us, every person he brings into our lives, is the perfect preparation for the future that only he can see.

Corrie ten Boom

Waiting is the hardest kind of work, but God knows best, and we may joyfully leave all in His hands.

Lottie Moon

God is God. He knows what he is doing. When you can't trace his hand, trust his heart.

Max Lucado

He has the right to interrupt your life. He is Lord. When you accepted Him as Lord, you gave Him the right to help Himself to your life anytime He wants.

Henry Blackaby

Be diligent to present yourself approved to God, a worker who doesn't need to be ashamed, correctly teaching the word of truth.

2 Timothy 2:15 HCSB

Beyond Guilt

All of us have sinned. Sometimes our sins result from our own stubborn rebellion against God's commandments. And sometimes, we are swept up in events that are beyond our abilities to control. Under either set of circumstances, we may experience intense feelings of guilt. But God has an answer for the guilt that we feel. That answer, of course, is His forgiveness. When we confess our wrongdoings and repent from them, we are forgiven by the One who created us.

Are you troubled by feelings of guilt or regret? If so, you must repent from your misdeeds, and you must ask your Heavenly Father for His forgiveness. When you do so, He will forgive you completely and without reservation. Then, you must forgive yourself just as God has forgiven you: thoroughly and unconditionally.

More Great Ideas About Guilt

Spiritual life without guilt would be like physical life without pain. Guilt is a defense mechanism; it's like an alarm that goes off to lead you to confession when you sin.

John MacArthur

If God has forgiven you, why can't you forgive yourself?

Marie T. Freeman

One of Satan's most effective ploys is to make us believe that we are small, insignificant, and worthless.

Susan Lenzkes

Guilt is a healthy regret for telling God one thing and doing another.

Max Lucado

You never lose the love of God. Guilt is the warning that temporarily you are out of touch.

Jack Dominian

I the Lord do not change.

Malachi 3:6 HCSB

What Doesn't Change

We live in a world that is always changing, but we worship a God who never changes—thank goodness! That means that we can be comforted in the knowledge that our Heavenly Father is the rock that simply cannot be moved.

The next time you face difficult circumstances, tough times, unfair treatment, or unwelcome changes, remember that some things never change—things like the love that you feel in your heart for your family and friends . . . and the love that God feels for you. So, instead of worrying too much about life's inevitable challenges, focus your energies on finding solutions. Have faith in your own abilities, do your best to solve your problems, and leave the rest up to God.

More Great Ideas About Change

Some of us seem so anxious about avoiding hell that we forget to celebrate our journey toward heaven.

Philip Yancey

God has a course mapped out for your life, and all the inadequacies in the world will not change His mind. He will be with you every step of the way. And though it may take time, He has a celebration planned for when you cross over the "Red Seas" of your life.

Charles Swindoll

How much of our lives are, well, so daily. How often our hours are filled with the mundane, seemingly unimportant things that have to be done, whether at home or work. These very "daily" tasks could become a celebration of praise. "It is through consecration," someone has said, "that drudgery is made divine."

Gigi Graham Tchividjian

The main joy of heaven will be the heavenly Father greeting us in a time and place of rejoicing, celebration, joy, and great reunion.

Bill Bright

Both a good marriage and a bad marriage have moments of struggle, but in a healthy relationship, the husband and wife search for answers and areas of agreement because they love each other.

James Dobson

The fewer words, the better prayer.

Martin Luther

Part of good communication is listening with the eyes as well as with the ears.

Josh McDowell

In terms of the parable of the Prodigal Son, repentance is the flight home that leads to joyful celebration. It opens the way to a future, to a relationship restored.

Philip Yancey

When we are young, change is a treat, but as we grow older, change becomes a threat. But when Jesus Christ is in control of your life, you need never fear change or decay.

Warren Wiersbe

The fear of the Lord is the beginning of wisdom, and the knowledge of the Holy One is understanding.

Proverbs 9:10 HCSB

The Right Kind of Fear

Do you have a healthy, fearful respect for God's power? If so, you are both wise and obedient. And, because you are a thoughtful believer, you also understand that genuine wisdom begins with a profound appreciation for God's limitless power.

God praises humility and punishes pride. That's why God's greatest servants will always be those humble men and women who care less for their own glory and more for God's glory. In God's kingdom, the only way to achieve greatness is to shun it. And the only way to be wise is to understand these facts: God is great; He is all-knowing; and He is all-powerful. We must respect Him, and we must humbly obey His commandments, or we must accept the consequences of our misplaced pride.

More Great Ideas About Fearing God

If we do not tremble before God, the world's system seems wonderful to us and pleasantly consumes us.

James Montgomery Boice

A healthy fear of God will do much to deter us from sin.

Charles Swindoll

When true believers are awed by the greatness of God and by the privilege of becoming His children, then they become sincerely motivated, effective evangelists.

Bill Hybels

The remarkable thing about fearing God is that when you fear God, you fear nothing else, whereas if you do not fear God, you fear everything else.

Oswald Chambers

It is not possible that mortal men should be thoroughly conscious of the divine presence without being filled with awe.

C. H. Spurgeon

A merry heart does good, like medicine.

Proverbs 17:22 NKJV

Cheerfulness Is a Gift

Cheerfulness is a gift that we give to others and to ourselves. And, as believers who have been saved by a risen Christ, why shouldn't we be cheerful? The answer, of course, is that we have every reason to honor our Savior with joy in our hearts, smiles on our faces, and words of celebration on our lips.

Few things in life are more sad, or, for that matter, more absurd, than grumpy Christians. Christ promises us lives of abundance and joy if we accept His love and His grace. Yet sometimes, even the most righteous among us are beset by fits of ill temper and frustration. During these moments, we may not feel like turning our thoughts and prayers to Christ, but if we seek to gain perspective and peace, that's precisely what we must do.

Are you a cheerful Christian? You should be! And what is the best way to attain the joy that is rightfully yours? By giving Christ what is rightfully His: your heart, your soul, and your life.

More Great Ideas About Cheerfulness

God is good, and heaven is forever. And if those two facts don't cheer you up, nothing will.

Marie T. Freeman

Sour godliness is the devil's religion.

John Wesley

Christ can put a spring in your step and a thrill in your heart. Optimism and cheerfulness are products of knowing Christ.

Billy Graham

The people whom I have seen succeed best in life have always been cheerful and hopeful people who went about their business with a smile on their faces.

Charles Kingsley

We may run, walk, stumble, drive, or fly, but let us never lose sight of the reason for the journey, or miss a chance to see a rainbow on the way.

Gloria Gaither

Be assured, my dear friend, that it is no joy to God in seeing you with a dreary countenance.

C. H. Spurgeon

My cup runs over. Surely goodness and mercy shall follow me all the days of my life; and I will dwell in the house of the Lord Forever.

Psalm 23:5-6 NKJV

Optimistic Christianity

Pessimism and Christianity don't mix. Why? Because Christians have every reason to be optimistic about life here on earth and life eternal. As C. H. Spurgeon observed, "Our hope in Christ for the future is the mainstream of our joy." But sometimes, we fall prey to worry, frustration, anxiety, or sheer exhaustion, and our hearts become heavy. What's needed is plenty of rest, a large dose of perspective, and God's healing touch, but not necessarily in that order.

Today, make this promise to yourself and keep it: vow to be a hope-filled Christian. Think optimistically about your life, your profession, your future, and your family. Trust your hopes, not your fears. Take time to celebrate God's glorious creation. And then, when you've filled your heart with hope and gladness, share your optimism with others. They'll be better for it, and so will you. But not necessarily in that order.

More Great Ideas About Optimism

The Christian lifestyle is not one of legalistic do's and don'ts, but one that is positive, attractive, and joyful.

Vonette Bright

The popular idea of faith is of a certain obstinate optimism: the hope, tenaciously held in the face of trouble, that the universe is fundamentally friendly and things may get better.

J. I. Packer

The essence of optimism is that it takes no account of the present, but it is a source of inspiration, of vitality, and of hope. Where others have resigned, it enables a man to hold his head high, to claim the future for himself, and not abandon it to his enemy.

Dietrich Bonhoeffer

The people whom I have seen succeed best in life have always been cheerful and hopeful people who went about their business with a smile on their faces.

Charles Kingsley

It is a remarkable thing that some of the most optimistic and enthusiastic people you will meet are those who have been through intense suffering.

Warren Wiersbe

Christ can put a spring in your step and a thrill in your heart. Optimism and cheerfulness are products of knowing Christ.

Billy Graham

Developing a positive attitude means working continually to find what is uplifting and encouraging.

Barbara Johnson

Keep your feet on the ground, but let your heart soar as high as it will. Refuse to be average or to surrender to the chill of your spiritual environment.

A. W. Tozer

If our hearts have been attuned to God through an abiding faith in Christ, the result will be joyous optimism and good cheer.

Billy Graham

But grow in the grace and knowledge of our Lord and Savior Jesus Christ. To Him be the glory both now and forever.

2 Peter 3:18 NKJV

Spiritual Growth

The words of 2 Peter 3:18 make it clear: spiritual growth is a journey, not a destination. When it comes to your faith, God doesn't intend for you to stand still; He wants you to keep moving and growing. In fact, God's plan for you includes a lifetime of prayer, praise, and spiritual growth.

Many of life's most important lessons are painful to learn. During times of heartbreak and hardship, we must be courageous and we must be patient, knowing that in His own time, God will heal us if we invite Him into our hearts.

Spiritual growth need not take place only in times of adversity. We must seek to grow in our knowledge and love of the Lord every day that we live. In those quiet moments when we open our hearts to God, the One who made us keeps remaking us. He gives us direction, perspective, wisdom, and courage. The appropriate moment to accept those spiritual gifts is the present one.

Are you as mature as you're ever going to be? Hopefully not! When it comes to your faith, God doesn't intend for you to become "fully grown," at least not in this lifetime. In fact, God still has important lessons that He intends to teach you. So ask yourself this: what lesson is God trying to teach me today? And then go about the business of learning it.

We often become mentally and spiritually barren because we're so busy.

—

Franklin Graham

More Great Ideas About Spiritual Growth

If all struggles and sufferings were eliminated, the spirit would no more reach maturity than would the child.

Elisabeth Elliot

We look at our burdens and heavy loads, and we shrink from them. But, if we lift them and bind them about our hearts, they become wings, and on them we can rise and soar toward God.

Mrs. Charles E. Cowman

The vigor of our spiritual lives will be in exact proportion to the place held by the Bible in our lives and in our thoughts.

George Mueller

A person who gazes and keeps on gazing at Jesus becomes like him in appearance.

E. Stanley Jones

We set our eyes on the finish line, forgetting the past, and straining toward the mark of spiritual maturity and fruitfulness.

Vonette Bright

But those who wait on the Lord shall renew their strength;
they shall mount up with wings like eagles, they shall run and
not be weary, they shall walk and not faint.

Isaiah 40:31 NKJV

Strength from God

Even the most inspired Christians can, from time to time, find themselves running on empty. The demands of daily life can drain us of our strength and rob us of the joy that is rightfully ours in Christ. When we find ourselves tired, discouraged, or worse, there is a source from which we can draw the power needed to recharge our spiritual batteries. That source is God.

God intends that His children lead joyous lives filled with abundance and peace. But sometimes, abundance and peace seem very far away. It is then that we must turn to God for renewal, and when we do, He will restore us if we allow Him to do so.

Today, like every other day, is literally brimming with possibilities. Whether we realize it or not, God is always working in us and through us; our job is to let Him do His work without undue interference. Yet we are imperfect beings who, because of our limited vision, often resist God's will. And oftentimes, because of our stubborn insistence on squeezing too many activities into a 24-hour day, we allow ourselves to become exhausted, or frustrated, or both.

Are you tired or troubled? Turn your heart toward God in prayer. Are you weak or worried? Take the time—or, more accurately, make the time—to delve deeply into God's Holy Word. Are you spiritually depleted? Call upon fellow believers to support you, and call upon Christ to renew your spirit and your life. Are you simply overwhelmed by the demands of the day? Pray for the wisdom to simplify your life. Are you exhausted? Pray for the wisdom to rest a little more and worry a little less.

When you do these things, you'll discover that the Creator of the universe stands always ready and always able to create a new sense of wonderment and joy in you.

We have a God who delights in impossibilities.

—

Andrew Murray

More Great Ideas About Strength

No matter how heavy the burden, daily strength is given, so I expect we need not give ourselves any concern as to what the outcome will be. We must simply go forward.

Annie Armstrong

When we spend time with Christ, He supplies us with strength and encourages us in the pursuit of His ways.

Elizabeth George

A divine strength is given to those who yield themselves to the Father and obey what He tells them to do.

Warren Wiersbe

The same God who empowered Samson, Gideon, and Paul seeks to empower my life and your life, because God hasn't changed.

Bill Hybels

One reason so much American Christianity is a mile wide and an inch deep is that Christians are simply tired. Sometimes you need to kick back and rest for Jesus' sake.

Dennis Swanberg

On the first day of the week, very early in the morning, they came to the tomb, bringing the spices they had prepared. They found the stone rolled away from the tomb. They went in but did not find the body of the Lord Jesus. While they were perplexed about this, suddenly two men stood by them in dazzling clothes. So the women were terrified and bowed down to the ground. "Why are you looking for the living among the dead?" asked the men. "He is not here, but He has been resurrected!"

Luke 24:1-6 HCSB

Considering the Resurrection

When we consider the resurrection of Christ, we marvel at God's power, His love, and His mercy. And if God is for us, what can we possibly have to fear? The answer, of course, is that those who have been saved by our living Savior have absolutely nothing to fear.

As we consider the meaning of Christ's life, His death, and His resurrection, we are reminded that God's most precious gift, His only Son, went to Calvary as a sacrifice for a sinful world. May we, as believers who have been saved by the blood of Christ, trust the promises of our Savior. And may we honor Him with our words, our deeds, our thoughts, and our prayers—not only today but also throughout all eternity.

More Great Ideas About the Resurrection

The Resurrection was a proclamation that Christ had conquered sin, death, and the devil. It guarantees there is life beyond the grave.

Charles Stanley

Our Lord has written the promise of the resurrection not in words alone, but in every leaf in springtime.

Martin Luther

The resurrection of Jesus, the whole alphabet of human hope, the certificate of our Lord's mission from heaven, is the heart of the gospel in all ages.

R. G. Lee

The resurrection of Jesus Christ is the power of God to change history and to change lives.

Bill Bright

The world has never been stable. Jesus Himself was born into the cruelest and most unstable of worlds. No, we have babies and keep trusting and living because the Resurrection is true! The Resurrection was not just a one-time event in history; it is a principle built into the very fabric of our beings, a fact reverberating from every cell of creation: Life wins! Life wins!

Gloria Gaither

The stone was rolled away from the tomb not so Jesus could get out, but so that the world could look in. His resurrection assures yours. Because He lives, you will live forever.

Charles Stanley

The power of the resurrection of Jesus Christ is a power that could overcome every spiritual failing, every sin, every weakness, in one explosive act.

Bill Hybels

The Resurrection is the biggest news in history. CNN ought to put it on Headline News every thirty minutes. It should scream from every headline: Jesus is alive!

Dennis Swanberg

Do not love the world or the things in the world. If anyone loves the world, the love of the Father is not in him.

1 John 2:15 NKJV

The World's Treasures or God's Treasures?

All of mankind is engaged in a colossal, worldwide treasure hunt. Some folks seek treasure from earthly sources, treasures such as material wealth or public acclaim; others seek God's treasures by making Him the cornerstone of their lives.

What kind of treasure hunter are you? Are you so caught up in the demands of popular society that you sometimes allow the search for worldly treasures to become your primary focus? If so, it's time to reorganize your daily to-do list by placing God in His rightful place: first place.

If you sincerely seek to strengthen your character, you'll focus more intently on God's treasures and less intently on the world's treasures. Don't allow anyone or anything to separate you from your Heavenly Father and His only begotten Son.

Society's priorities are transitory; God's priorities are permanent. The world's treasures are difficult to find and difficult to keep; God's treasures are ever-present and ev-erlasting. Which treasures and whose priorities will you claim as your own? The answer should be obvious.

Aim at heaven and you will
get earth thrown in;
aim at earth and you will
get neither.

—

C. S. Lewis

More Great Ideas About Worldliness

Our fight is not against any physical enemy; it is against organizations and powers that are spiritual. We must struggle against sin all our lives, but we are assured we will win.

Corrie ten Boom

As we have by faith said no to sin, so we should by faith say yes to God and set our minds on things above, where Christ is seated in the heavenlies.

Vonette Bright

The true Christian, though he is in revolt against the world's efforts to brainwash him, is no mere rebel for rebellion's sake. He dissents from the world because he knows that it cannot make good on its promises.

A. W. Tozer

Every day, I find countless opportunities to decide whether I will obey God and demonstrate my love for Him or try to please myself or the world system. God is waiting for my choices.

Bill Bright

The Lord bless you and keep you; the Lord make His face shine upon you, and be gracious to you.

Numbers 6:24-25 NKJV

Counting Your Blessings

If you sat down and began counting your blessings, how long would it take? A very, very long time! Your blessings include life, freedom, family, friends, talents, and possessions, for starters. But, your greatest blessing—a gift that is yours for the asking—is God's gift of salvation through Christ Jesus.

Today, begin making a list of your blessings. You most certainly will not be able to make a complete list, but take a few moments and jot down as many blessings as you can. Then give thanks to the giver of all good things: God. His love for you is eternal, as are His gifts. And it's never too soon—or too late—to offer Him thanks.

More Great Ideas About Blessings

When you and I are related to Jesus Christ, our strength and wisdom and peace and joy and love and hope may run out, but His life rushes in to keep us filled to the brim. We are showered with blessings, not because of anything we have or have not done, but simply because of Him.

Anne Graham Lotz

Do we not continually pass by blessings innumerable without notice, and instead fix our eyes on what we feel to be our trials and our losses, and think and talk about these until our whole horizon is filled with them, and we almost begin to think we have no blessings at all?

Hannah Whitall Smith

God blesses us in spite of our lives and not because of our lives.

Max Lucado

God's kindness is not like the sunset—brilliant in its intensity, but dying every second. God's generosity keeps coming and coming and coming.

Bill Hybels

God is more anxious to bestow His blessings on us than we are to receive them.

St. Augustine

Think of the blessings we so easily take for granted: Life itself; preservation from danger; every bit of health we enjoy; every hour of liberty; the ability to see, to hear, to speak, to think, and to imagine all this comes from the hand of God.

Billy Graham

Get rich quick! Count your blessings!

Anonymous

Jesus intended for us to be overwhelmed by the blessings of regular days. He said it was the reason he had come: "I am come that they might have life, and that they might have it more abundantly."

Gloria Gaither

The key to a blessed life is to have a listening heart that longs to know what the Lord is saying.

Jim Cymbala

Then He said to Thomas, "Put your finger here and observe My hands. Reach out your hand and put it into My side. Don't be an unbeliever, but a believer."

John 20:27 HCSB

Actions and Beliefs

Our theology must be demonstrated, not only by our words but, more importantly, by our actions. As Christians, we must do our best to make sure that our actions are accurate reflections of our beliefs. In short, we should be practical believers, quick to act whenever we see an opportunity to serve God.

We may proclaim our beliefs to our hearts' content, but our proclamations will mean nothing—to others or to ourselves—unless we accompany our words with deeds that match. The sermons that we live are far more compelling than the ones we preach. So remember this: whether you like it or not, your life is an accurate reflection of your creed. If this fact gives you cause for concern, don't bother talking about the changes that you intend to make—make them. And then, when your good deeds speak for themselves—as they most certainly will—don't interrupt.

More Great Ideas About Belief

The reason many of us do not ardently believe in the gospel is that we have never given it a rigorous testing, thrown our hard questions at it, or faced it with our most prickly doubts.

Eugene Peterson

I believe in Christ as I believe in that the Sun has risen, not only because I see it, but because by it I see everything else.

C. S. Lewis

We must understand that the first and chief thing—for everyone who would do the work of Jesus—is to believe, and in doing so, to become linked to Him, the Almighty One, and then to pray the prayer of faith in His Name.

Andrew Murray

What I believe about God is the most important thing about me.

A. W. Tozer

God delights to meet the faith of one who looks up to Him and says, "Lord, You know that I cannot do this—but I believe that You can!"

Amy Carmichael

For I am the Lord, I do not change.

Malachi 3:6 NKJV

He Does Not Change

Our world is in a state of constant change. God is not. At times, the world seems to be trembling beneath our feet. But we can be comforted in the knowledge that our Heavenly Father is the rock that cannot be shaken. His Word promises, "I am the Lord, I do not change."

Every day that we live, we mortals encounter a multitude of changes—some good, some not so good. And on occasion, all of us must endure life-changing personal losses that leave us heartbroken. When we do, our Heavenly Father stands ready to comfort us, to guide us, and—in time—to heal us.

Is the world spinning a little too fast for your liking? Are you facing difficult circumstances or unwelcome changes? If so, please remember that God is far bigger than any problem you may face. So, instead of worrying about life's inevitable challenges, put your faith in the Father and His only begotten Son. After all, "Jesus Christ is the same yesterday, today, and forever" (Hebrews 13:8 NKJV). And it is precisely because your

Savior does not change that you can face your challenges with courage for today and hope for tomorrow.

Are you anxious about situations that you cannot control? Take your anxieties to God. Are you troubled? Take your troubles to Him. Does your little corner of the universe seem to be trembling beneath your feet? Seek protection from the One who cannot be moved. The same God who created the universe will protect you if you ask Him . . . so ask Him . . . and then serve Him with willing hands and a trusting heart.

To God be the glory,
great things He has done;
So loved He the world
that He gave us His Son.

—

Fanny Crosby

More Great Ideas About God

We may blunder on for years thinking we know a great deal about Him, and then, perhaps suddenly, we catch a sight of Him as He is revealed in the face of Jesus Christ, and we discover the real God.

Hannah Whitall Smith

When all else is gone, God is still left. Nothing changes Him.

Hannah Whitall Smith

God can see clearly no matter how dark or foggy the night is. Trust His Word to guide you safely home.

Lisa Whelchel

God's actual divine essence and his will are absolutely beyond all human thought, human understanding or wisdom; in short, they are and ever will be incomprehensible, inscrutable, and altogether hidden to human reason.

Martin Luther

The God who dwells in heaven is willing to dwell also in the heart of the humble believer.

Warren Wiersbe

I lived with Indians who made pots out of clay which they used for cooking. Nobody was interested in the pot. Everybody was interested in what was inside. The same clay taken out of the same riverbed, always made in the same design, nothing special about it. Well, I'm a clay pot, and let me not forget it. But, the excellency of the power is of God and not us.

Elisabeth Elliot

God is the beyond in the midst of our life.

Dietrich Bonhoeffer

God is bigger than we can figure.

Criswell Freeman

God does not tell us what He is going to do; He reveals to us who He is.

Oswald Chambers

A man can no more diminish God's glory by refusing to worship Him than a lunatic can put out the sun by scribbling the word, "darkness" on the walls of his cell.

C. S. Lewis

You are the light of the world. A city that is set on a hill cannot be hidden. Nor do they light a lamp and put it under a basket, but on a lampstand, and it gives light to all who are in the house. Let your light so shine before men, that they may see your good works and glorify your Father in heaven.

Matthew 5:14-16 NKJV

You Are the Light

Matthew 5:14-16 makes it clear: Because you are a Christian, you are indeed "the light of the world." The Bible also says that you should live in a way that lets other people understand what it means to be a follower of Jesus.

Your personal testimony is profoundly important, but perhaps because of shyness (or because of the fear of being rebuffed), you've been hesitant to share your experiences. If so, you should start paying less attention to your own insecurities and more attention to the message that God wants you to share with the world.

Corrie ten Boom observed, "There is nothing anybody else can do that can stop God from using us. We can turn everything into a testimony." Her words remind us that when we speak up for God, our actions may speak even more loudly than our words.

When we let other people know the details of our faith, we assume an important responsibility: the responsibility of making certain that our words are reinforced by our actions. When we share our testimonies, we must also be willing to serve as shining examples of righteousness—undeniable examples of the changes that Jesus makes in the lives of those who accept Him as their Savior.

Are you willing to follow in the footsteps of Jesus? If so, you must also be willing to talk about Him. And make no mistake—the time to express your belief in Him is now. You know how He has touched your own heart; help Him do the same for others.

God has ordained that others
may see the reality of His presence by
the illumination our lives shed forth.

—

Beth Moore

More Great Ideas About Witnessing

We must go out and live among them, manifesting the gentle, loving spirit of our Lord. We need to make friends before we can hope to make converts.

Lottie Moon

If you are going to live in peace, you need to embrace in faith the reality that "the LORD is in His holy temple." Embrace it and be silent before Him. You don't need to argue. You don't need to defend God. Simply explain Him as the Word of God explains Him. Then it is the skeptic's responsibility to accept or reject the Word of God. The responsibility is his, not yours. It's between him and God. It's a matter of faith.

Kay Arthur

In your desire to share the gospel, you may be the only Jesus someone else will ever meet. Be real and be involved with people.

Barbara Johnson

There is no thrill quite as wonderful as seeing someone else come to trust Christ because I have been faithful in sharing the story of my own faith.

Vonette Bright

Every tiny bit of my life that has value I owe to the redemption of Jesus Christ. Am I doing anything to enable Him to bring His redemption into evident reality in the lives of others?

Oswald Chambers

Jesus' images portray the Kingdom as a kind of secret force. Sheep among wolves, treasure hidden in a field, the tiniest seed in a garden, wheat growing among weeds, a pinch of yeast worked into bread dough; all these hint at a movement that works within society, changing it from inside out.

Philip Yancey

When Christians live out their faith with authenticity and boldness, they put a little zing into a sometimes bland cup of soup. They catch people off guard and make them wince. They wake people up with their challenges and seemingly radical points of view. And, they overturn a few applecarts here and there.

Bill Hybels

Stay on the issue of Christ when witnessing, not the church, or denominations, or religion, or theological differences, or doctrinal questions. Speak precisely of Jesus, the Savior.

Charles Swindoll

I was glad when they said unto me, Let us go into the house of the LORD.

Psalm 122:1 KJV

Our Need to Worship God

All of humanity is engaged in worship. The question is not whether we worship, but what we worship. Wise men and women choose to worship God. When they do, they are blessed with a plentiful harvest of joy, peace, and abundance. Other people choose to distance themselves from God by foolishly worshiping things that are intended to bring personal gratification but not spiritual gratification. Such choices often have tragic consequences.

If we place our love for material possessions above our love for God—or if we yield to the countless temptations of this world—we find ourselves engaged in a struggle between good and evil, a clash between God and Satan. Our responses to these struggles have implications that echo throughout our families and throughout our communities.

How can we ensure that we cast our lot with God? We do so, in part, by the practice of regular, purposeful worship in the company of fellow believers. When we worship God faithfully and fervently, we are blessed. When we fail to worship God, for whatever reason, we forfeit the spiritual gifts that He intends for us.

We must worship our Heavenly Father, not just with our words, but also with deeds. We must honor Him, praise Him, and obey Him. As we seek to find purpose and meaning for our lives, we must first seek His purpose and His will. For believers, God comes first. Always first.

Do you place a high value on the practice of worship? Hopefully so. After all, every day provides countless opportunities to put God where He belongs: at the very center of your life. It's up to you to worship God seven days a week; anything less is simply not enough.

When God is at the center of your life, you worship. When he's not, you worry.

—

Rick Warren

More Great Ideas About Worship

God has promised to give you all of eternity. The least you can do is give Him one day a week in return.

Marie T. Freeman

In Biblical worship you do not find the repetition of a phrase; instead, you find the worshipers rehearsing the character of God and His ways, reminding Him of His faithfulness and His wonderful promises.

Kay Arthur

To worship Him in truth means to worship Him honestly, without hypocrisy, standing open and transparent before Him.

Anne Graham Lotz

In the sanctuary, we discover beauty: the beauty of His presence.

Kay Arthur

Worship is spiritual. Our worship must be more than just outward expression, it must also take place in our spirits.

Franklin Graham

Inside the human heart is an undeniable, spiritual instinct to commune with its Creator.

Jim Cymbala

Go, therefore, and make disciples of all nations, baptizing them in the name of the Father and of the Son and of the Holy Spirit, teaching them to observe everything I have commanded you. And remember, I am with you always, to the end of the age.

Matthew 28:19-20 HCSB

The Great Commission

Are you a bashful Christian, one who is afraid to speak up for your Savior? Do you leave it up to others to share their testimonies while you stand on the sidelines, reluctant to share yours? Too many of us are slow to obey the last commandment of the risen Christ; we don't do our best to "make disciples of all the nations."

Christ's Great Commission applies to Christians of every generation, including our own. As believers, we are commanded to share the Good News with our families, with our neighbors, and with the world. Jesus invited His disciples to become fishers of men. We, too, must accept the Savior's invitation, and we must do so today. Tomorrow may indeed be too late.

More Great Ideas About the Great Commission

Our commission is quite specific. We are told to be His witness to all nations. For us, as His disciples, to refuse any part of this commission frustrates the love of Jesus Christ, the Son of God.

Catherine Marshall

There are many timid souls whom we jostle morning and evening as we pass them by; but if only the kind word were spoken they might become fully persuaded.

Fanny Crosby

How many people have you made homesick for God?

Oswald Chambers

You cannot keep silent once you have experienced salvation of Jesus Christ.

Warren Wiersbe

To stand in an uncaring world and say, "See, here is the Christ" is a daring act of courage.

Calvin Miller

If we are ever going to be or do anything for our Lord, now is the time.

Vance Havner

Your light is the truth of the Gospel message itself as well as your witness as to Who Jesus is and what He has done for you. Don't hide it.

Anne Graham Lotz

There is nothing anybody else can do that can stop God from using us. We can turn everything into a testimony.

Corrie ten Boom

Choose Jesus Christ! Deny yourself, take up the Cross, and follow Him—for the world must be shown. The world must see, in us, a discernible, visible, startling difference.

Elisabeth Elliot

There is nothing more appealing or convincing to a watching world than to hear the testimony of someone who has just been with Jesus.

Henry Blackaby